A HALF-BAKED HISTORY OF

GINGERBREAD

Best Wishes

This book is dedicated
to everyone who has adopted
a gingerbread into their family.
Thank you for providing my
special biscuits with safe homes
and loving care. SJ

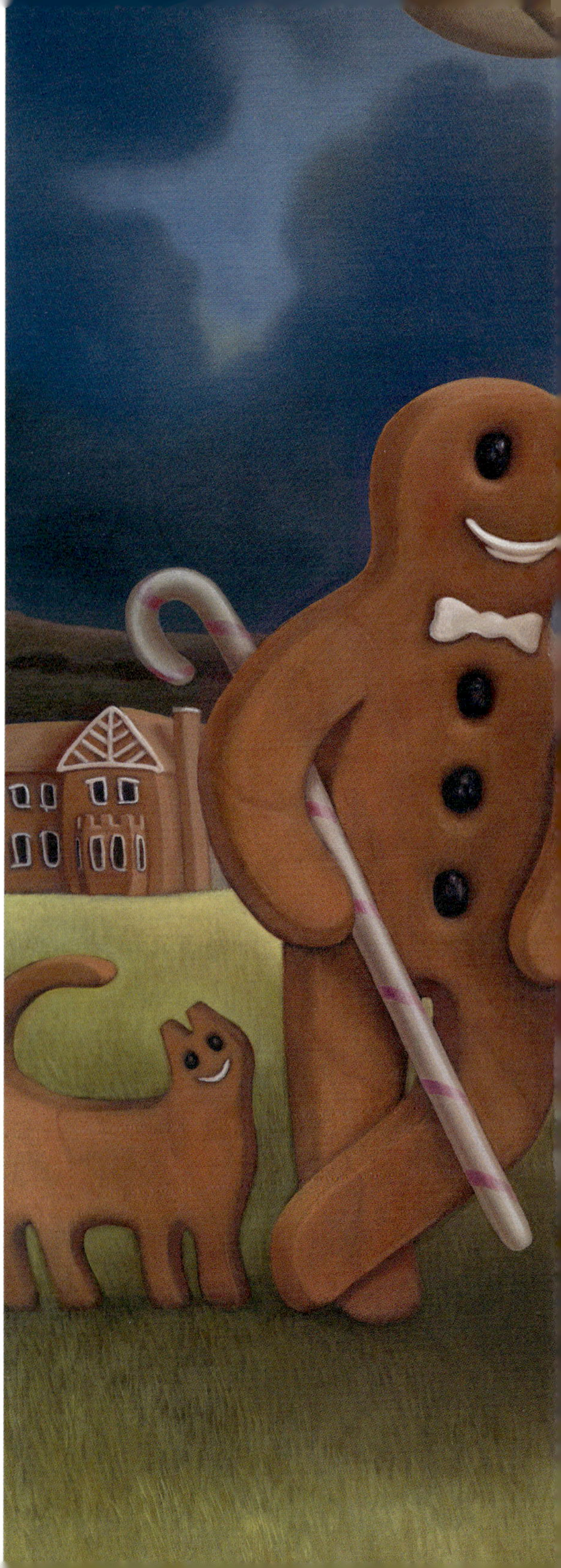

A HALF-BAKED HISTORY OF GINGERBREAD

BY SARAH-JANE SZIKORA

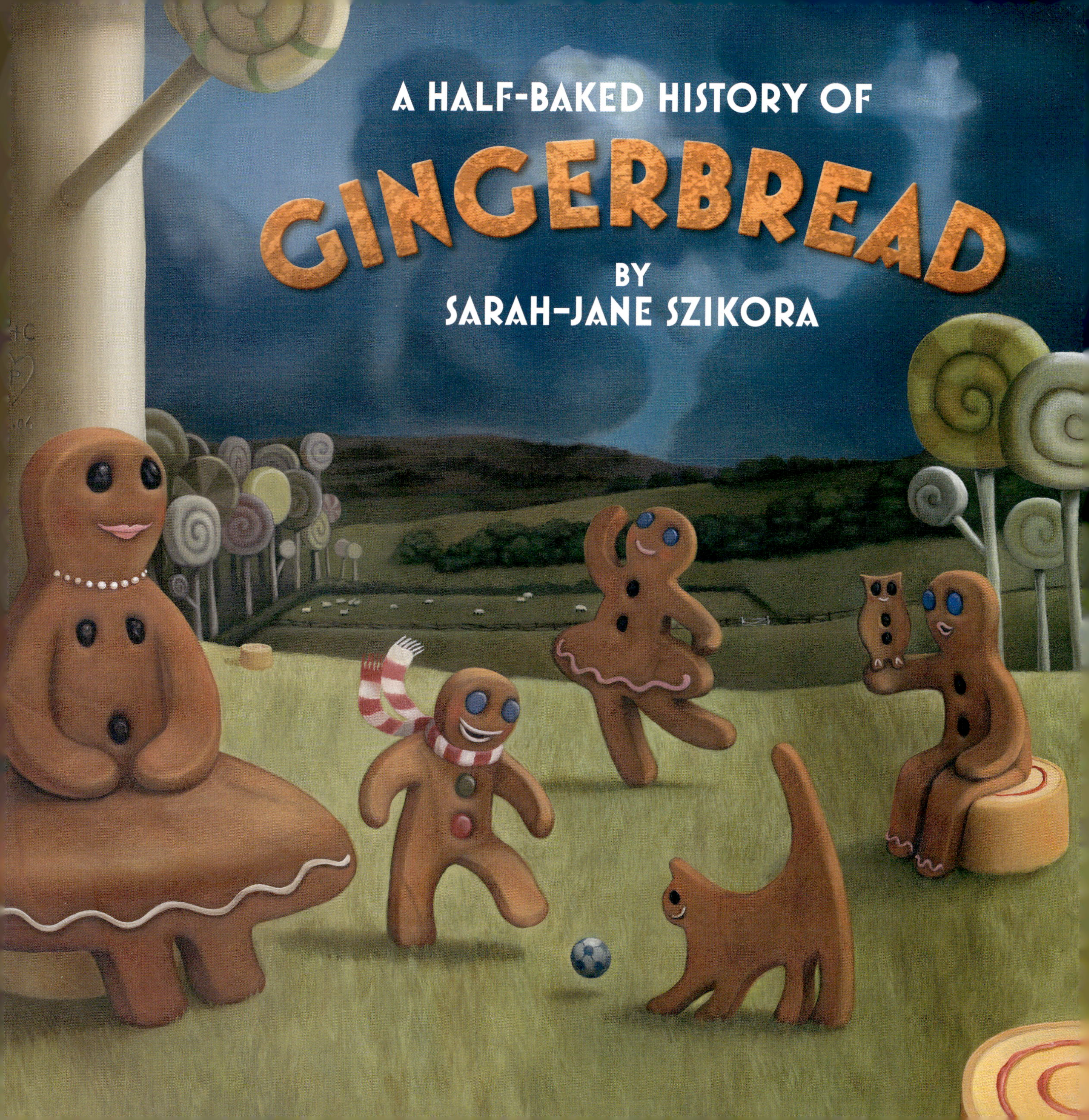

First published by SJ Szikora, 2015

A CIP catalogue record for this book is available from the British Library

ISBN 978-0-9932471-0-1

Designed by Guy Callaby (www.guycallaby.co.uk)
Edited by Jinny Johnson
Printed in the UK

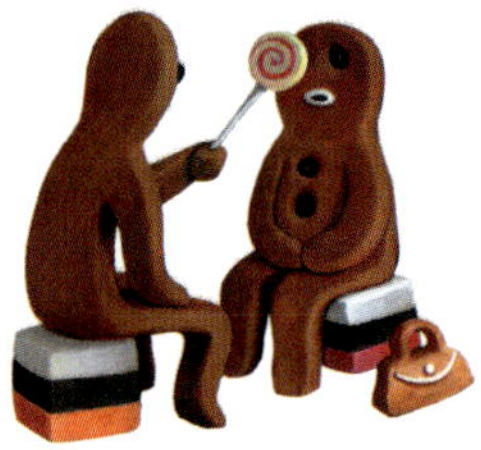

When I was unable to paint for a while after having eye surgery I had the idea for this book and put together a collection of existing paintings and drawings to tell the story of gingerbread. Although presented in a new context of 'history', each picture has its own story and personal significance.

My special thanks to Guy and Jinny for their wisdom and talents, and to Ian for being a constant support. SJ

INGREDIENTS

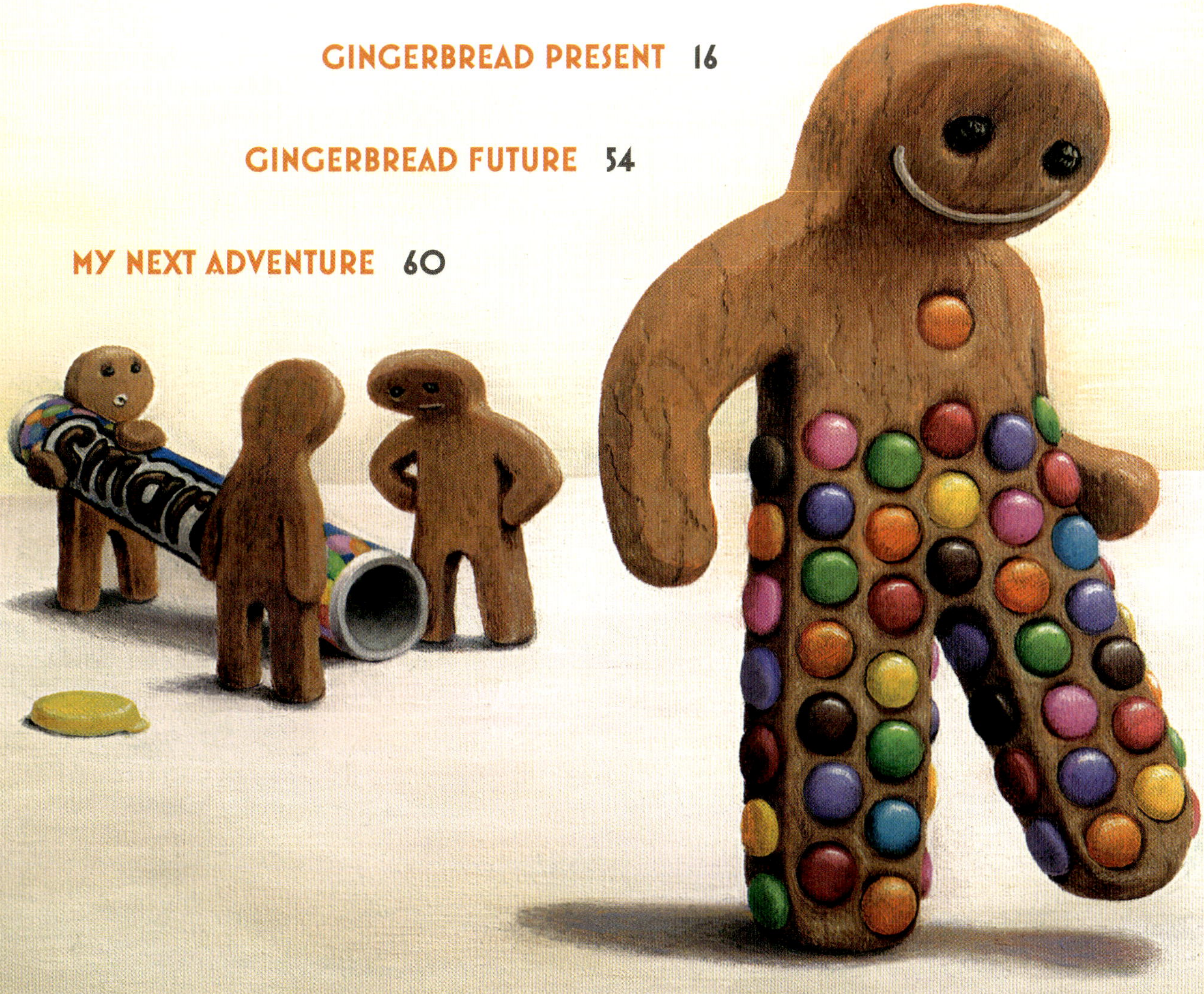

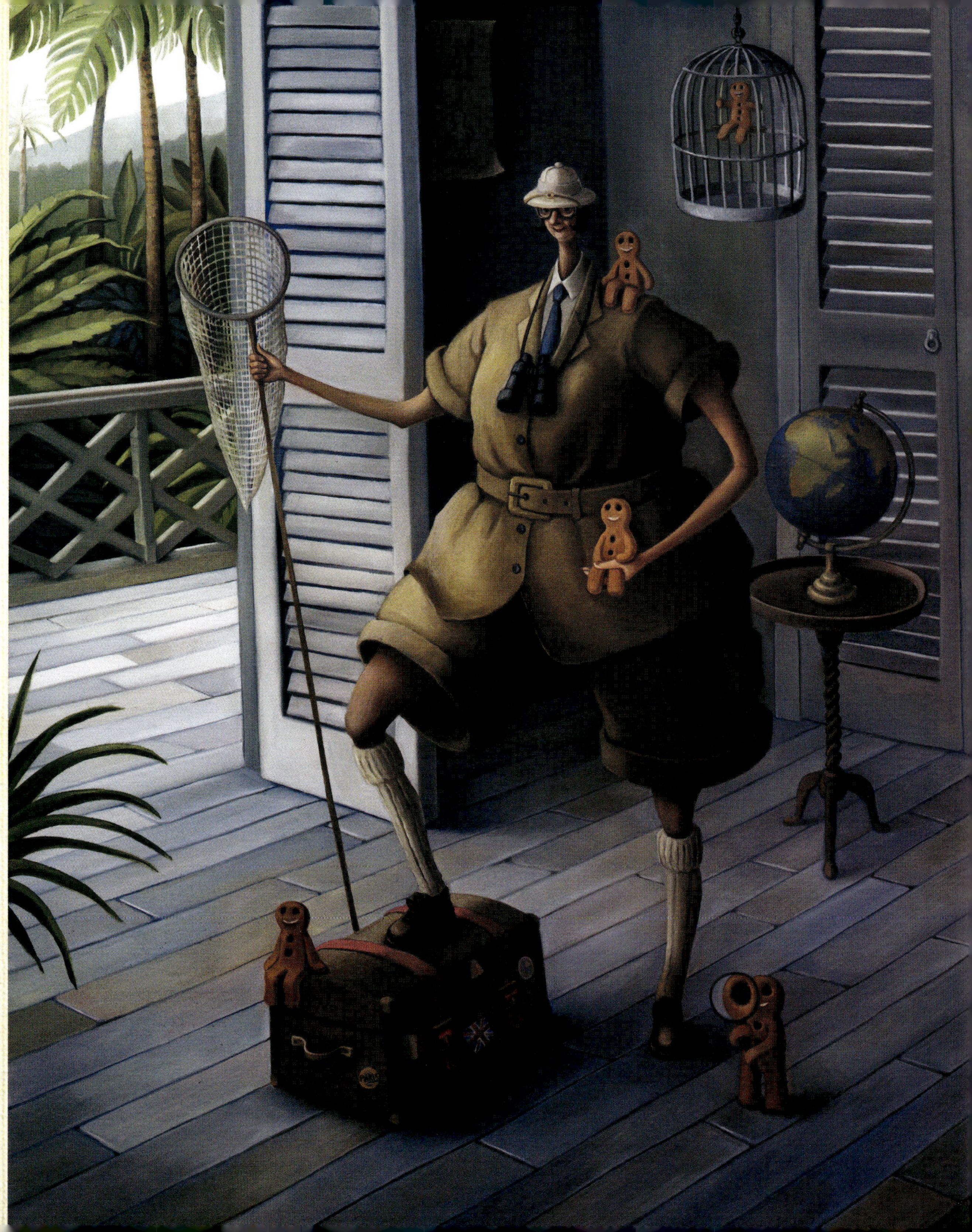

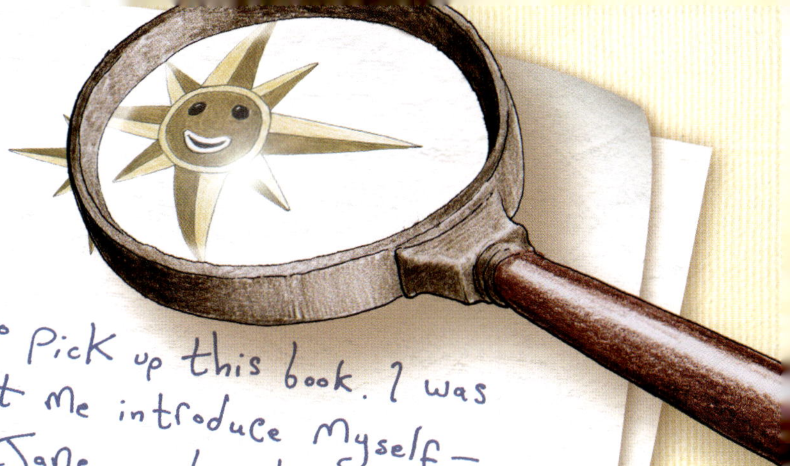

Dear Reader,

How splendid of you to pick up this book. I was hoping you might. Let me introduce myself – my name is Sarah-Jane, also known as Szikora the explorer. I am a biscologist and an artist; that is to say, I search for biscuits, gingerbread in particular, then I study and paint them.*

The observation and recording of gingerbread behaviour has been my life's work. Delving into the natural and social history of this special biscuit has meant years of hiding in bushes near their habitat and making peace offerings (icing bags mainly) to earn their trust.

This book contains a collection of pictures that illustrate my research into one of our planet's most secretive species.

If you'd like to step this way, I would be delighted to share with you what I have learned and show you how this delighful creature lives alongside us in the world today...

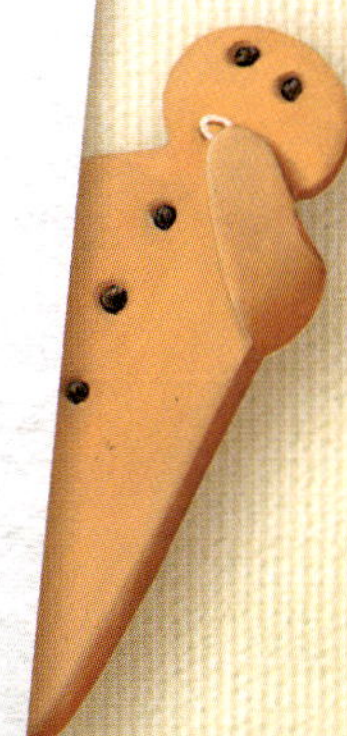

* any likeness to individual gingerbread living or dead is entirely coincidental.

GINGERBREAD PAST

Billions of years ago, a simple cell flobbered around in a pool of warm water. Eventually bits came off it and these turned into more cells. Over a very long time indeed, these weird blobs began to take the form of the living things that we know today: plants, fungi, insects, fish, reptiles, birds, mammals – even people.

Somewhere between the earliest mammals and the great apes, a unique little species arrived and began its own evolution. It began as a sort of orangey-coloured crumb and was to become what we now know as *Homo biscuitus* or Gingerbread Man.

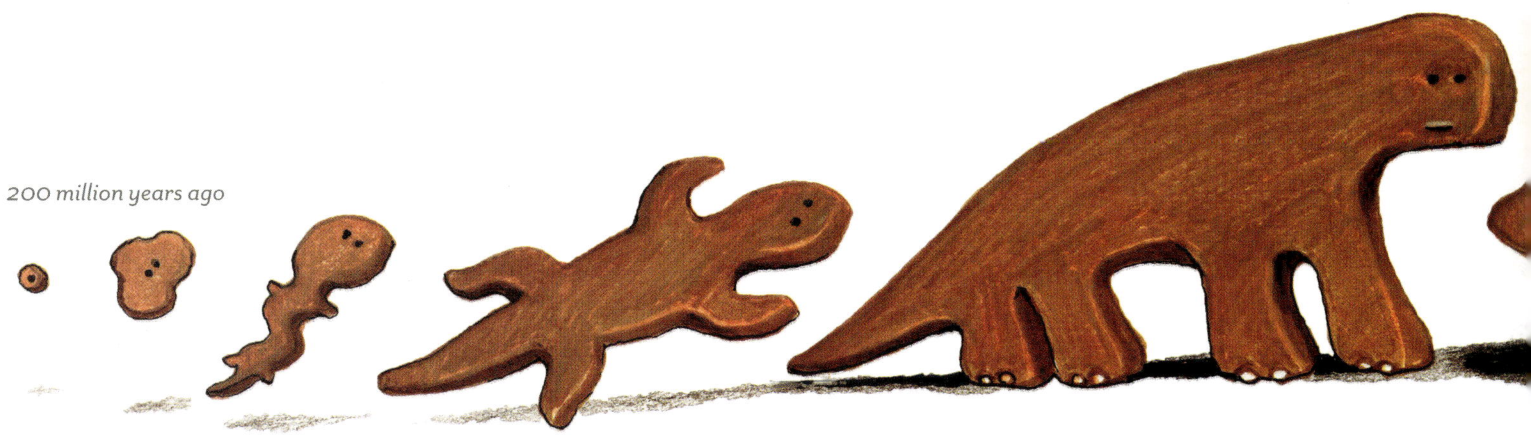

Homo biscuitus

20 million years ago

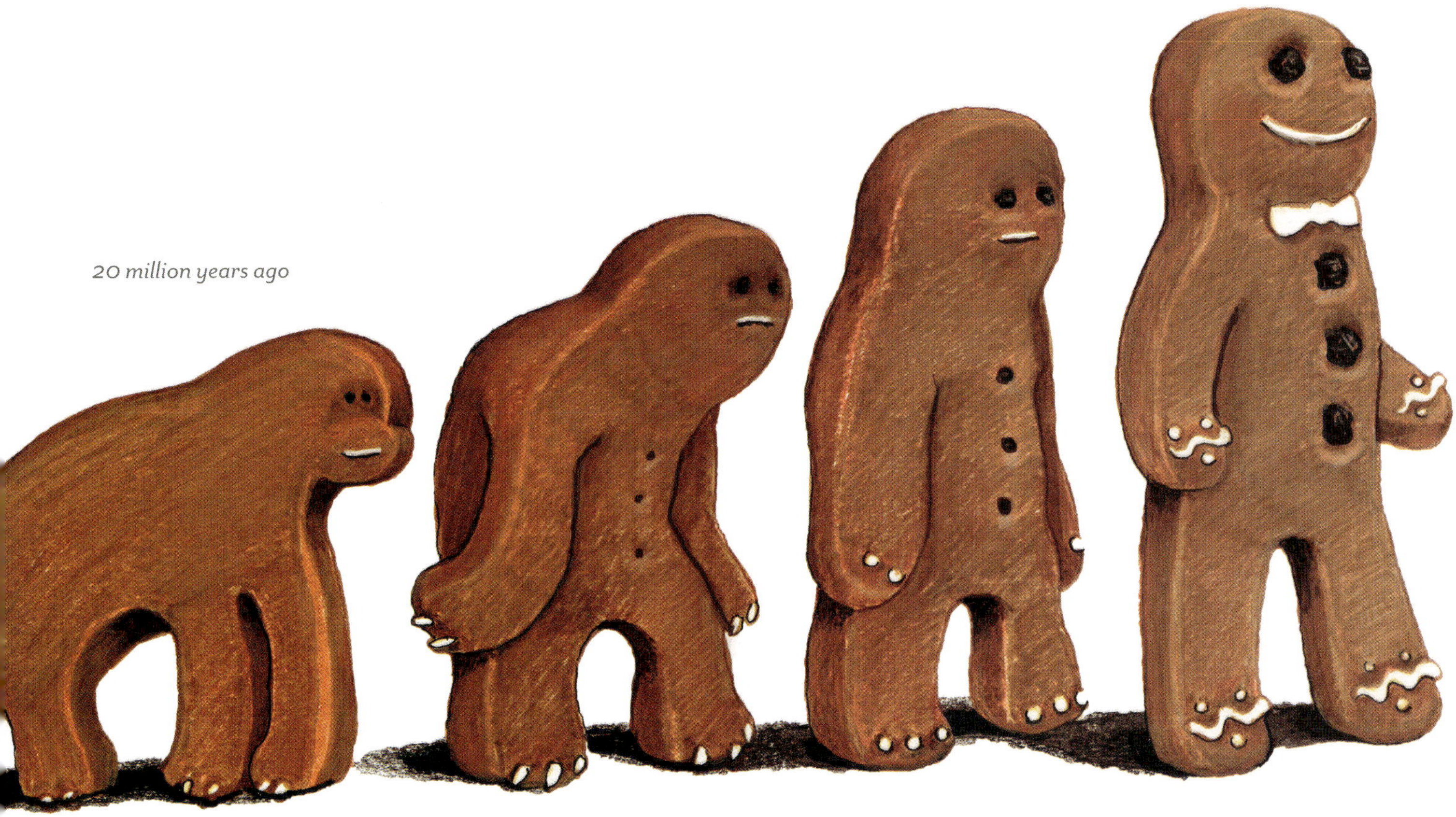

After a jolly good scout through the secret vaults of important museums around the world, I discovered that the first evidence of the existence of gingerbread came from the biblical era.

In the great flood of 2348 BC creatures of all shapes and sizes boarded the ark. Among them, almost unnoticed, were two small gingerbread.

How these two managed to survive is a mystery, but experts believe that Noah spent 40 days and 40 nights making cheese sandwiches to be sure that his passengers didn't eat each other.

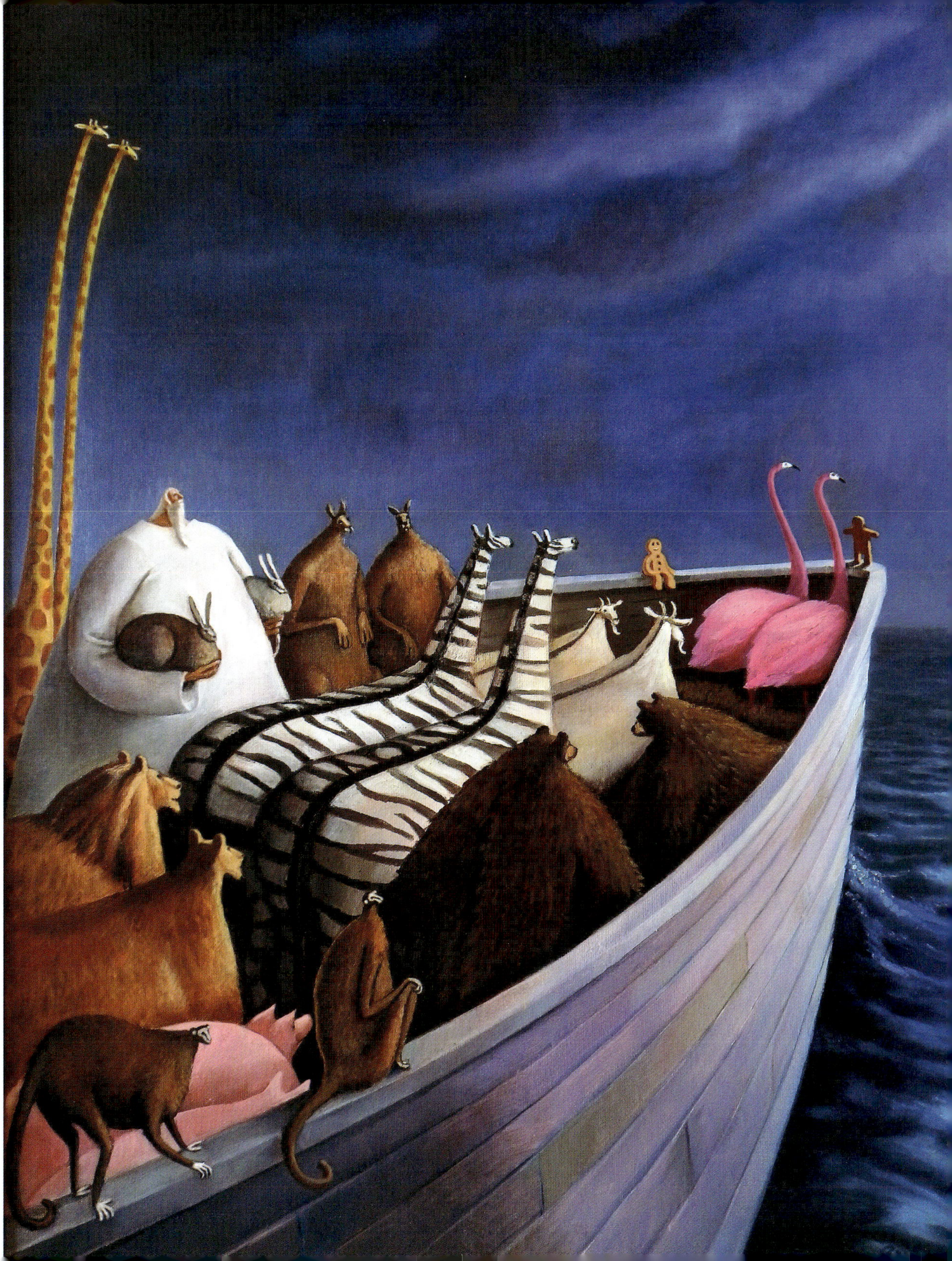

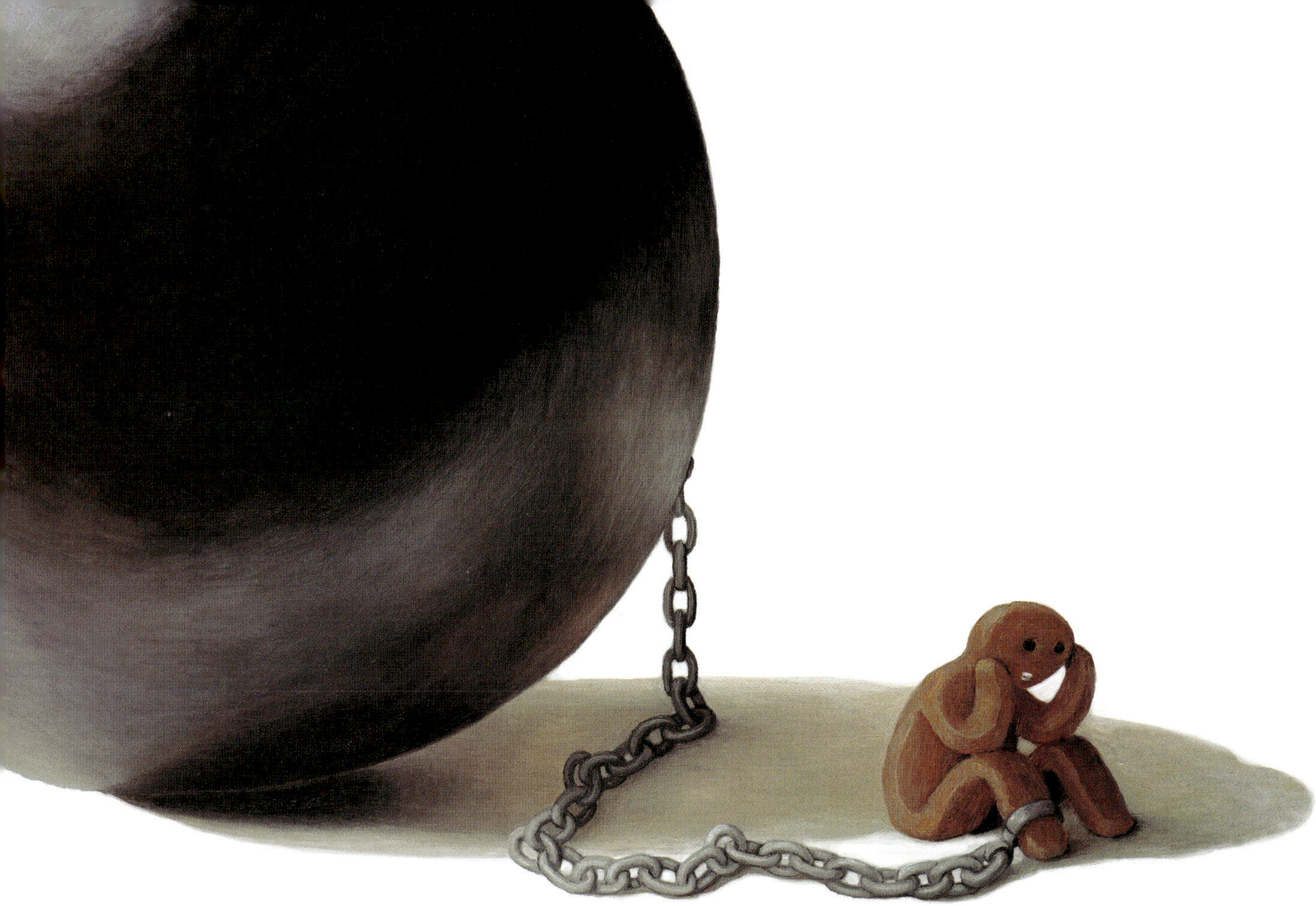

Natives of central Europe, gingerbread were present during the rise of the Roman Empire: 27 BC (before cake) – 330 AD (after doughnuts)

It was a turbulent time for biscuits and many were kept as slaves by wealthy Romans.

Some gingerbread won their freedom in ferocious battles at the Colosseum. They were forced to slay fellow gingerbread as well as scary lions and monsters, so they had to be brave. The crowds would go wild at the sight of the most famous gladiator, Biscuitus Maximus.

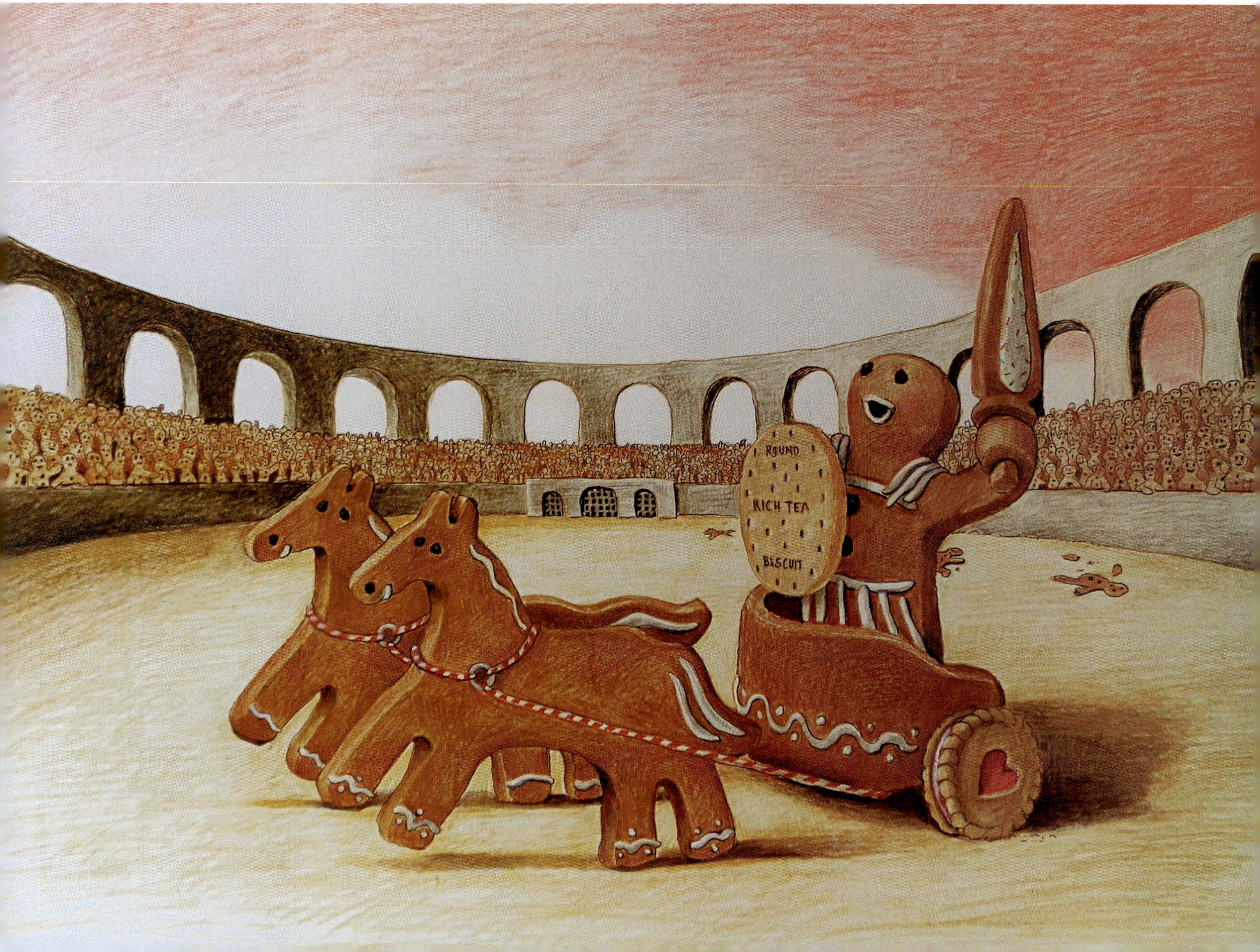

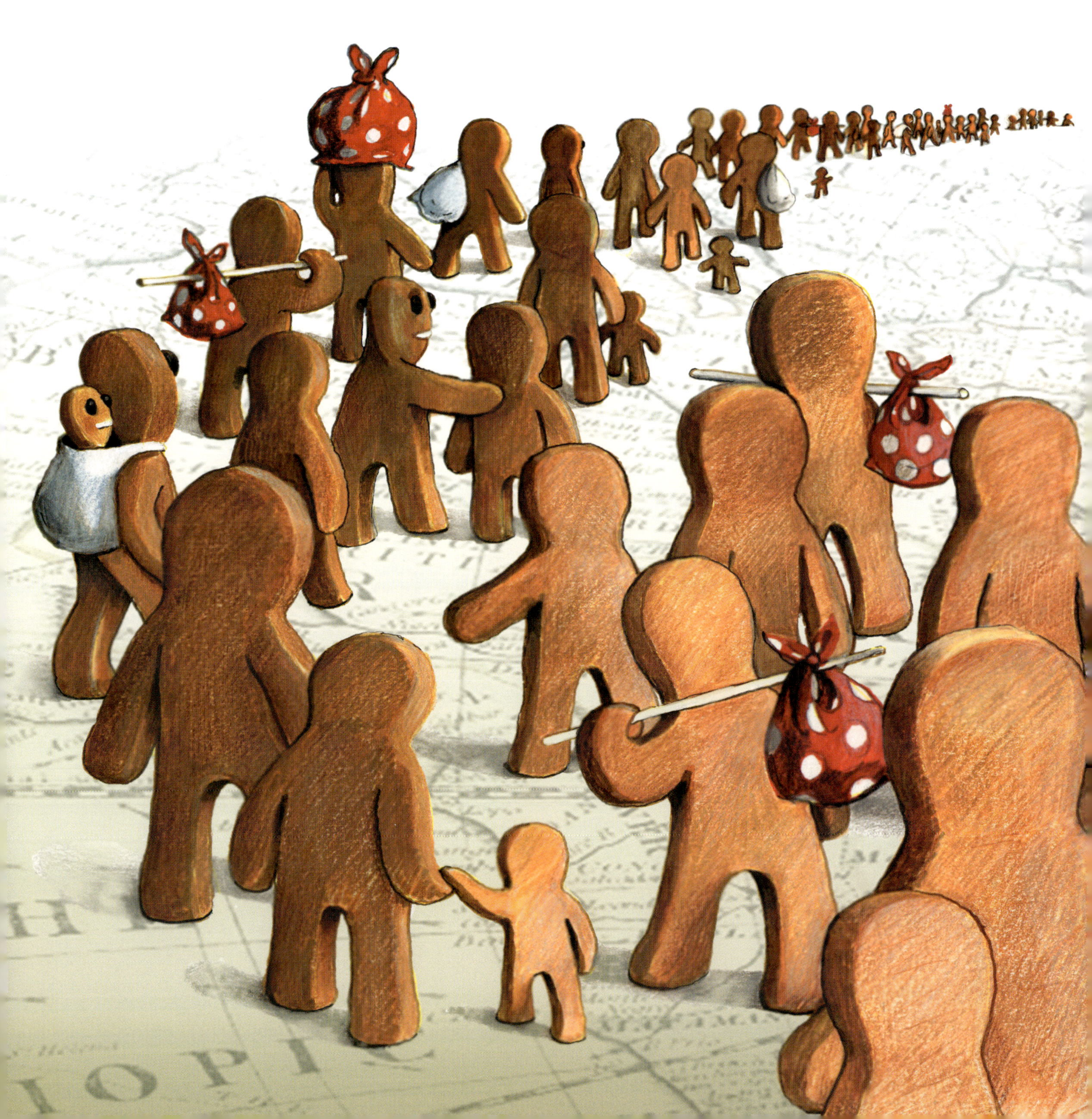

Following the collapse of the Roman Empire, and in fact all through history, there have been times of mass exodus, with biscuits leaving troubled lands in search of peace.

Not designed for walking hundreds or even thousands of miles, many migrating gingers would perish on their long journeys. Some would be eaten by predators, while others suffered terribly from 'crumblefoot', a horrid condition affecting weak and elderly biscuits.

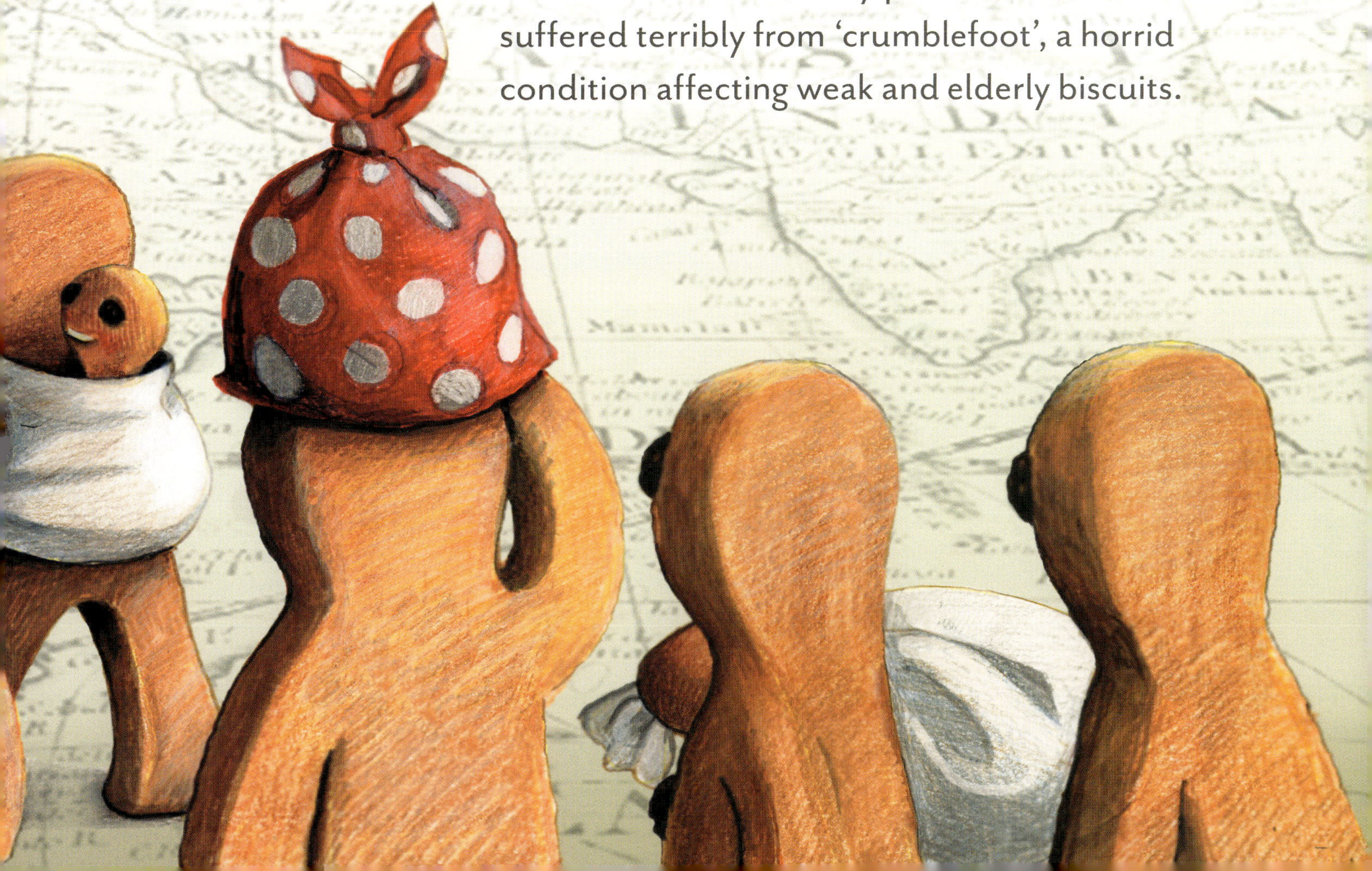

GINGERBREAD PRESENT

Born and Bread

Today, this species is mostly bred in captivity by humans to supply the delicious biscuit industry. However, gingerbread retain a strong survival instinct and will always attempt escape.

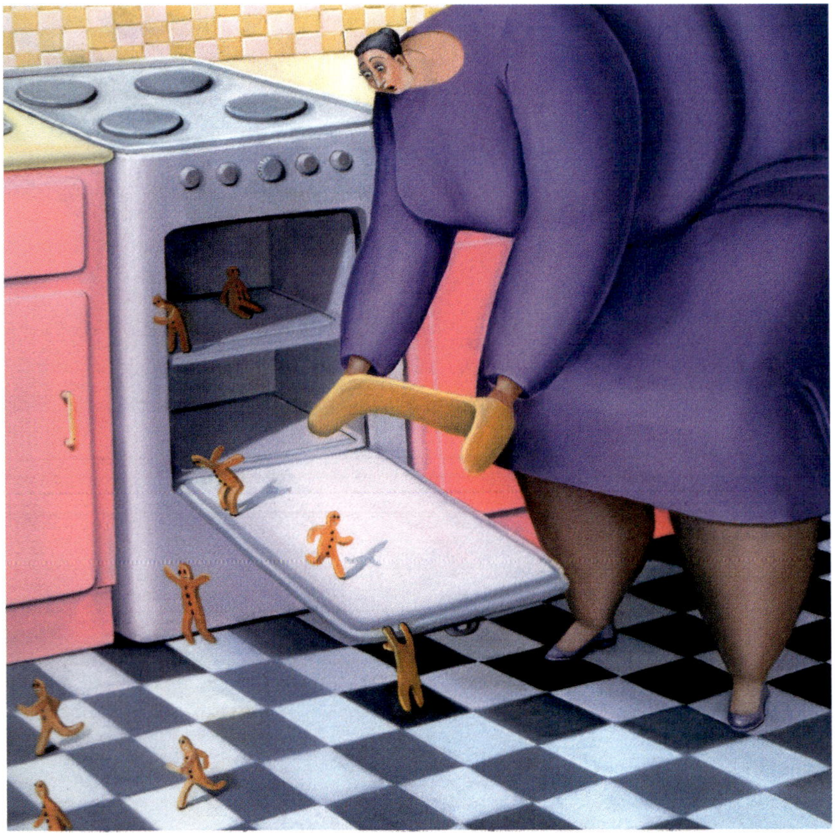

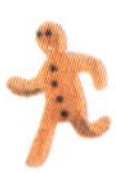

Sadly, wild gingerbread are no longer as plentiful as they once were. Hunting and the erosion of their natural habitat is causing a decline in numbers.

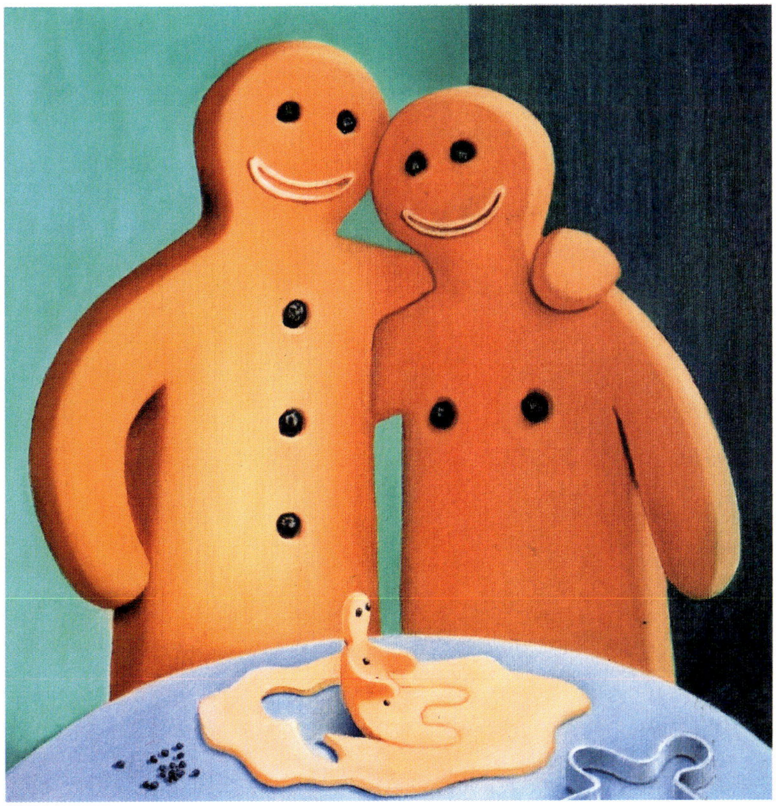

Thankfully, some biscuits are able to successfully procreate on their own.

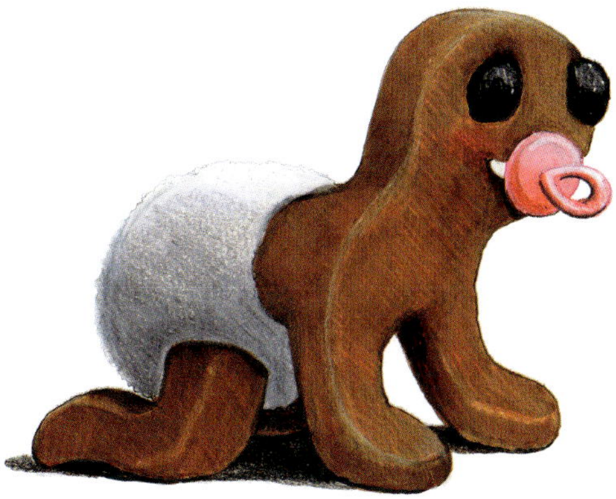

It's obvious why gingerbread are in need of protection. There is nothing in the world that's cuter or more mouthwatering than a baby biscuit – known as a rusk.

The life span of the average gingerbread is about one hour to eight weeks, though away from natural threats they can live much, much longer.

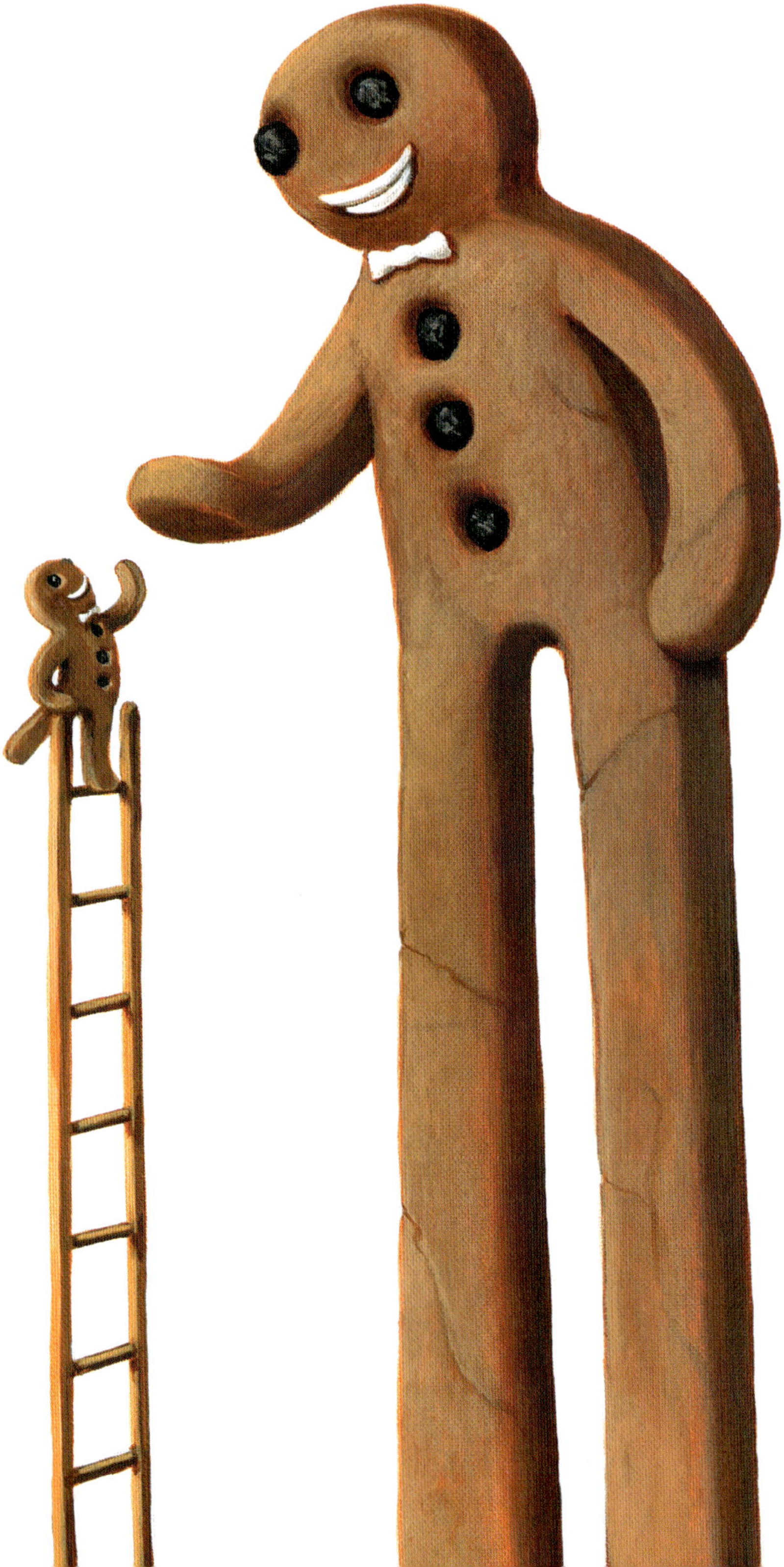

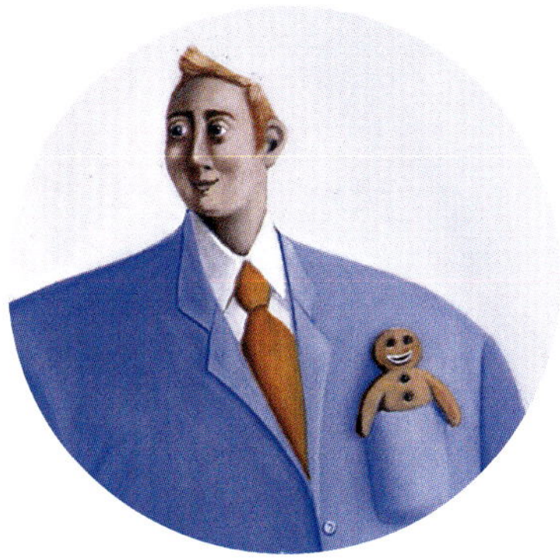

Gingerbread come in all shapes and sizes, from pocket-size to king-size. Americans are the largest. The world record was set in 1898 by a Texan biscuit who measured an incredible 7 feet, 3 inches tall!!

Once established, a family group tends to stay together.

For a while, I studied one family from Warwickshire, Mr and Mrs Button and their five children. It was fascinating to watch them work as a team and I noted how much they enjoyed each other's company. Mr Button, a gentle, kindly biscuit, told me how proud he was of his sons and daughters and how he hoped one day to be a grandbiscuit.

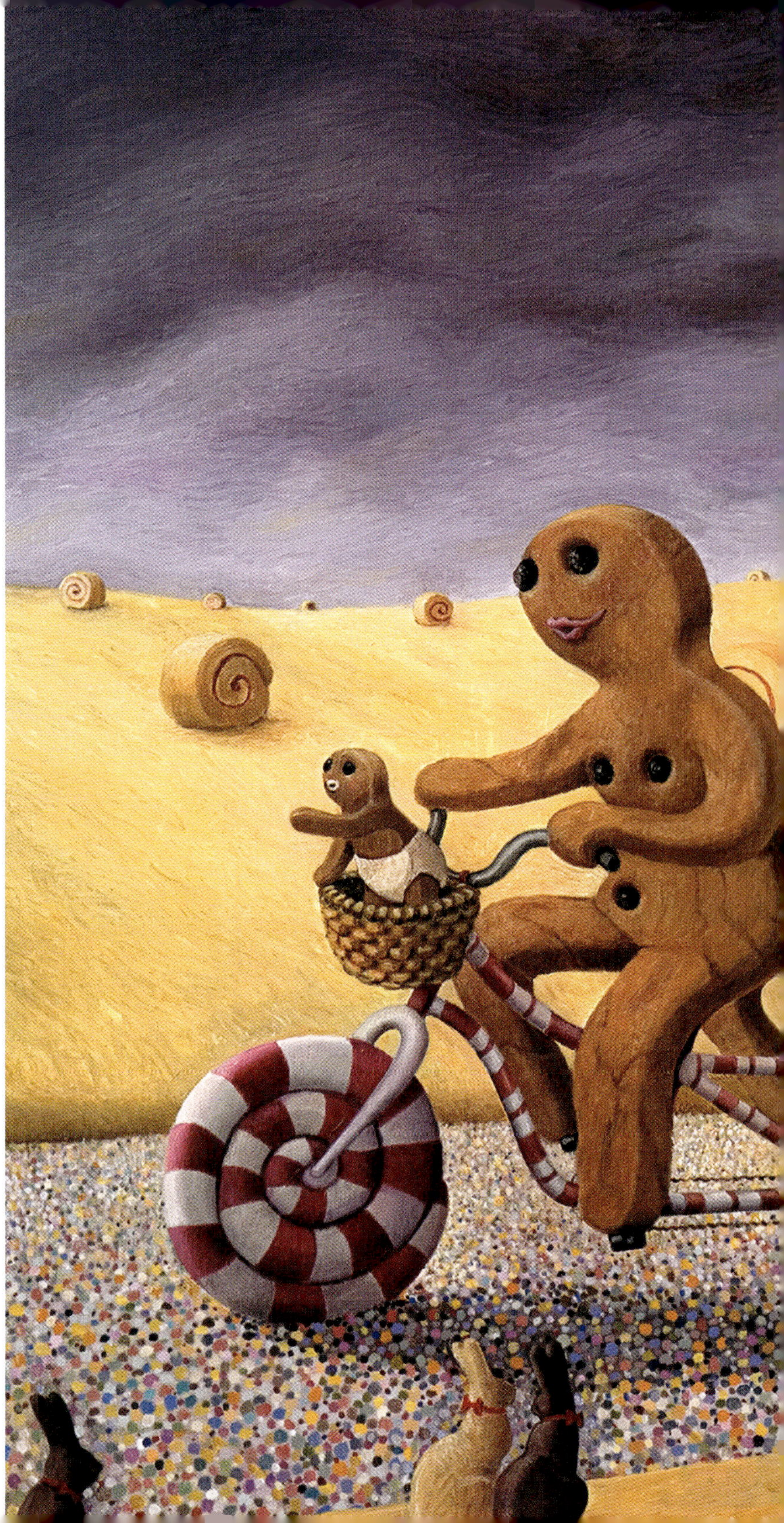

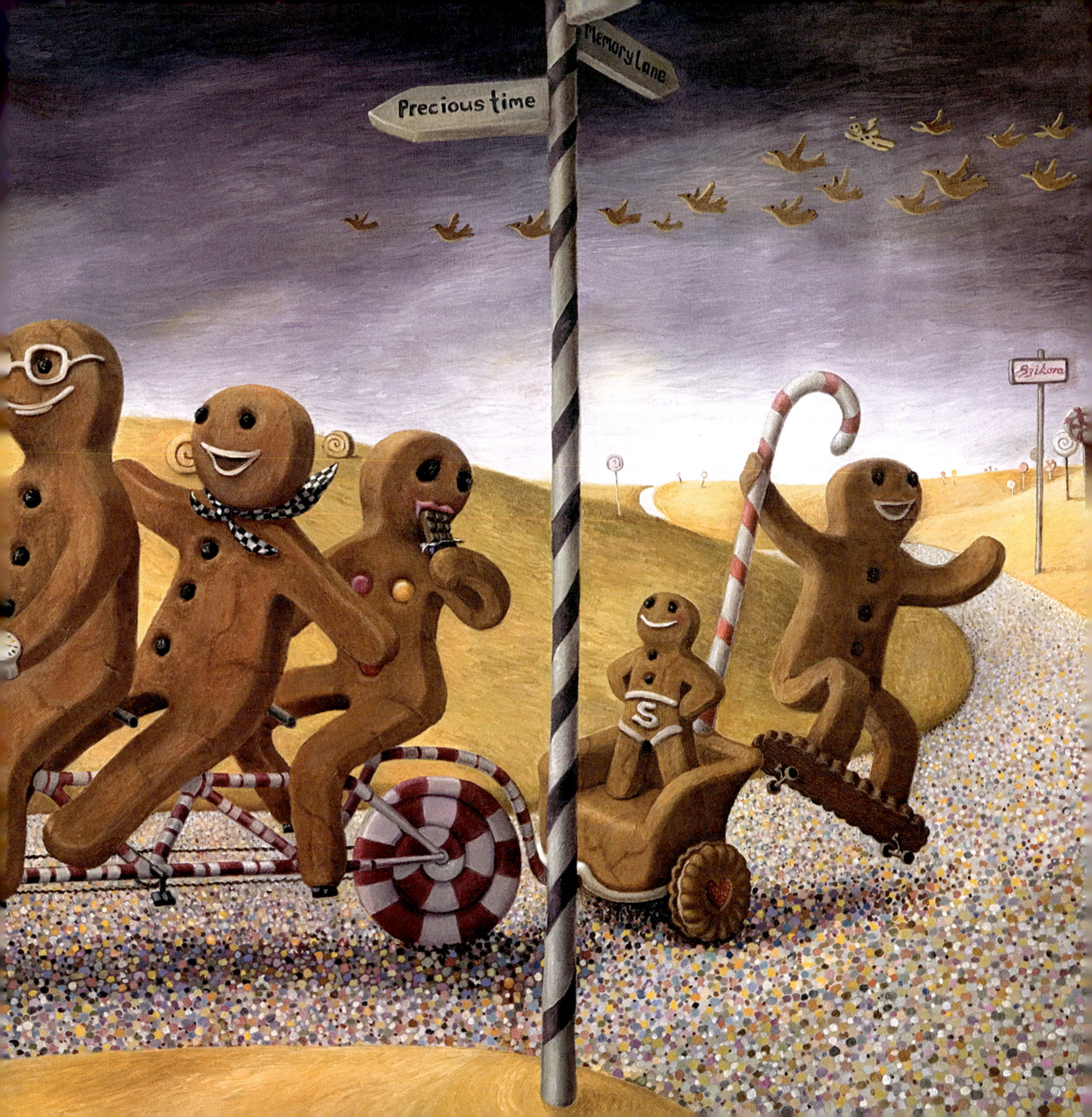
Precious time
Memory Lane

In a Custard Cream and Pleasant Land

Gingerbread born in captivity often live in cramped boxes and high-rise cupboards. Free-range biscuits are luckier. They live in peaceful, mature gingerbread properties with their extended families and dog biscuits.

I travelled round Tyneside one day with my paintbrush to observe gingerbread life in the street. I sat quietly behind some bins and managed to capture this heart-warming scene.

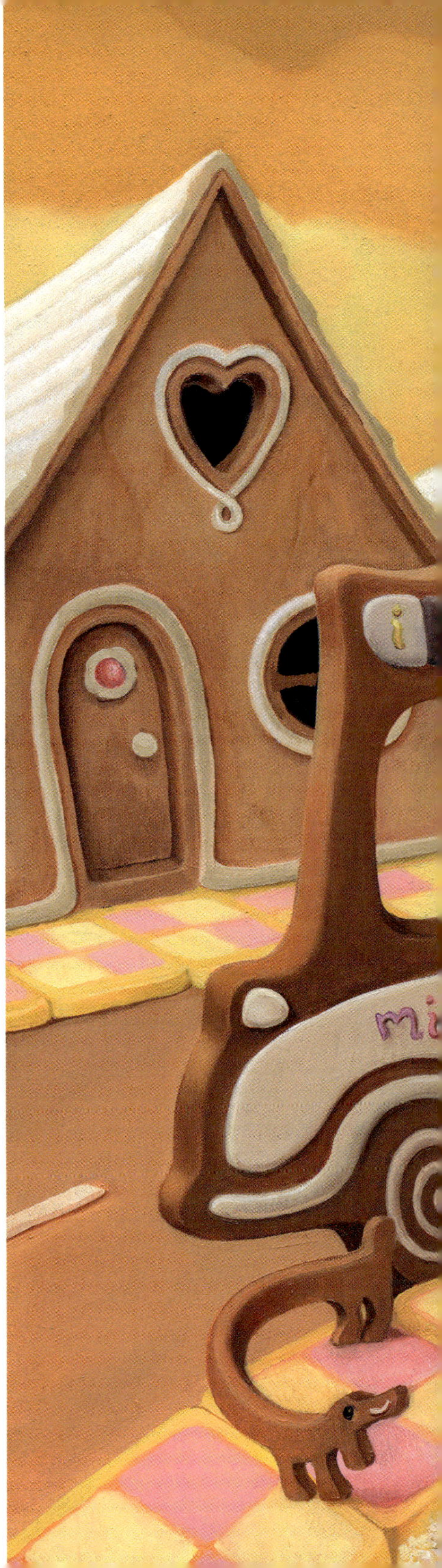

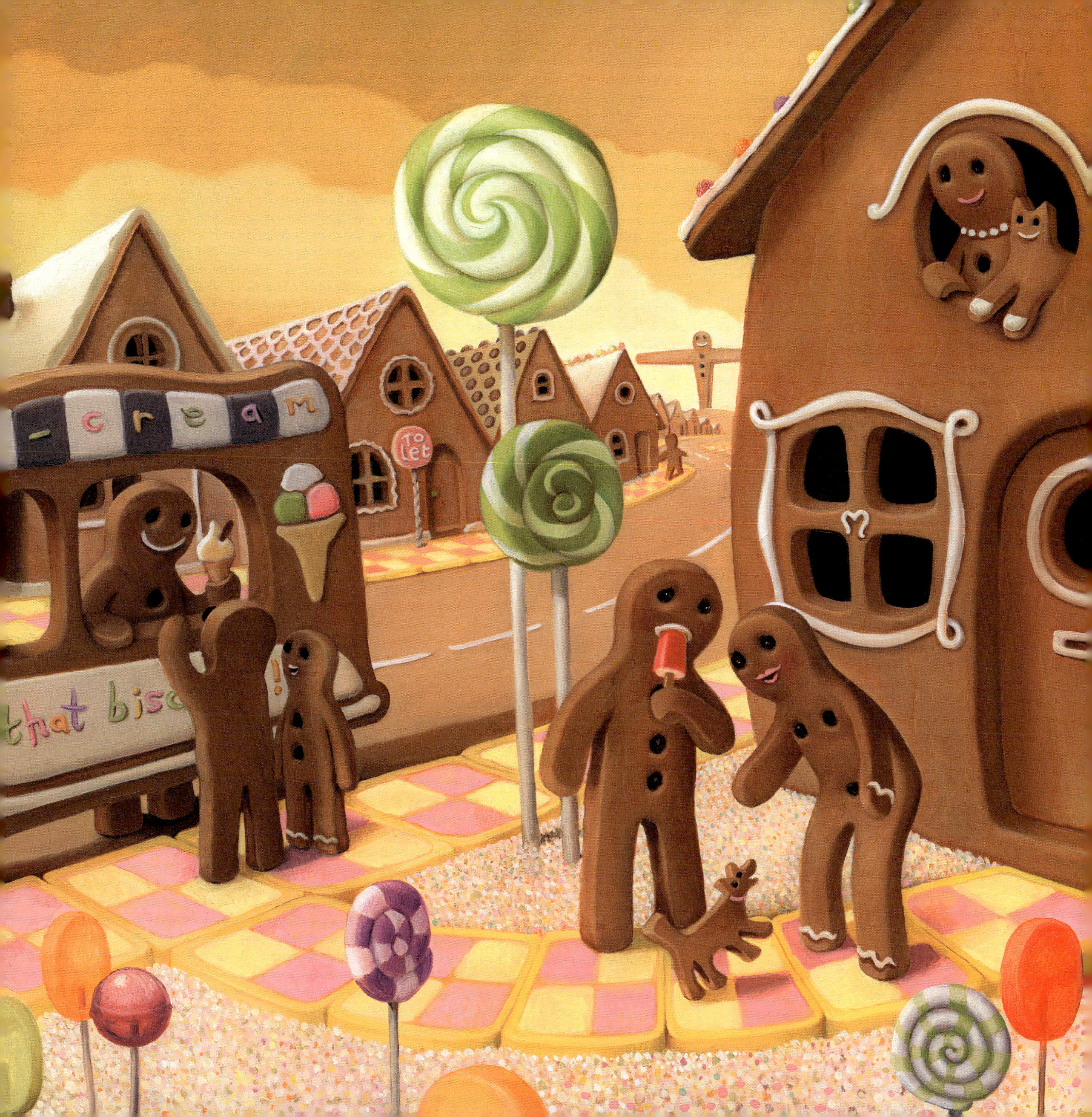
-cream
To let
that bisc

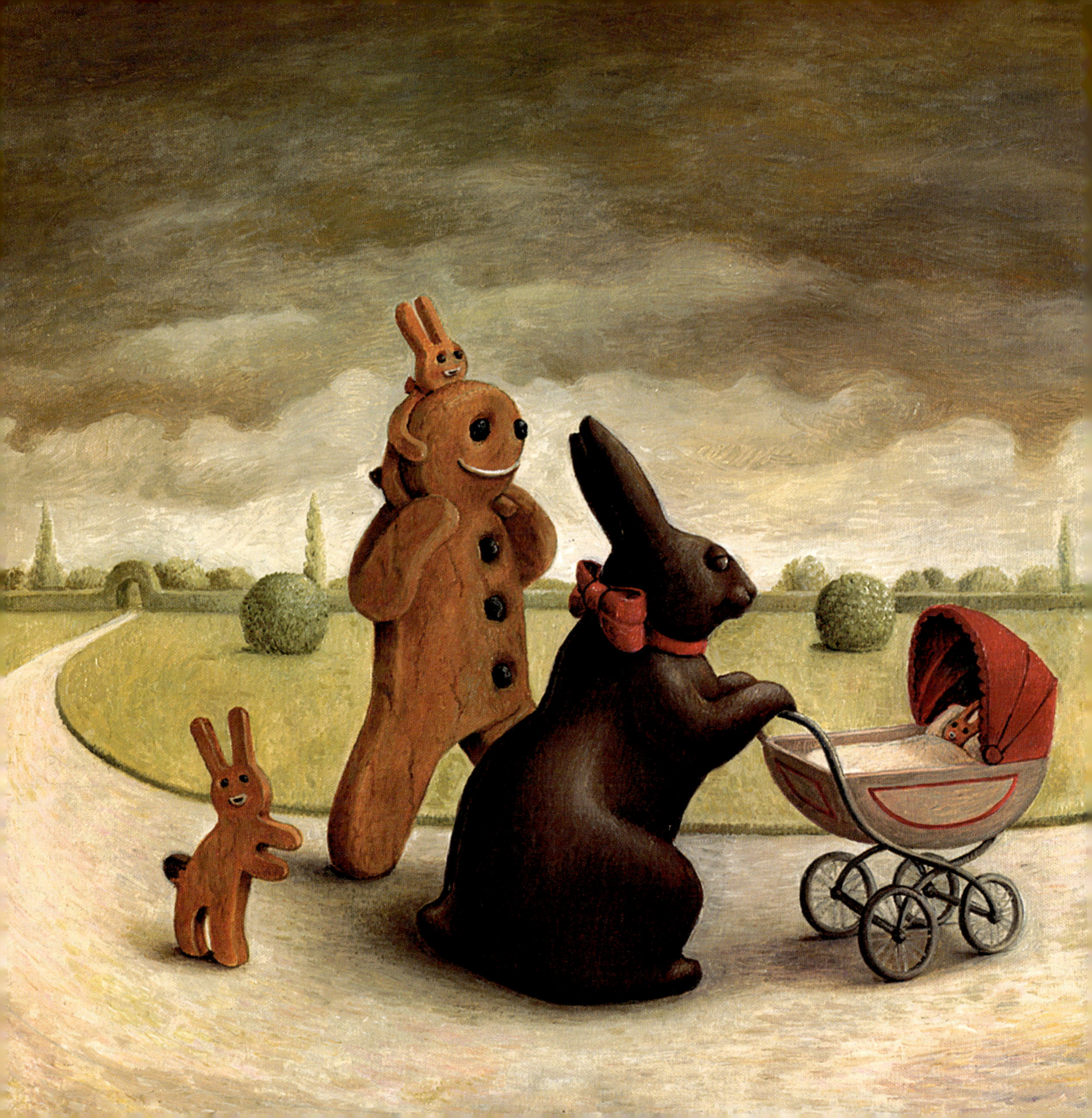

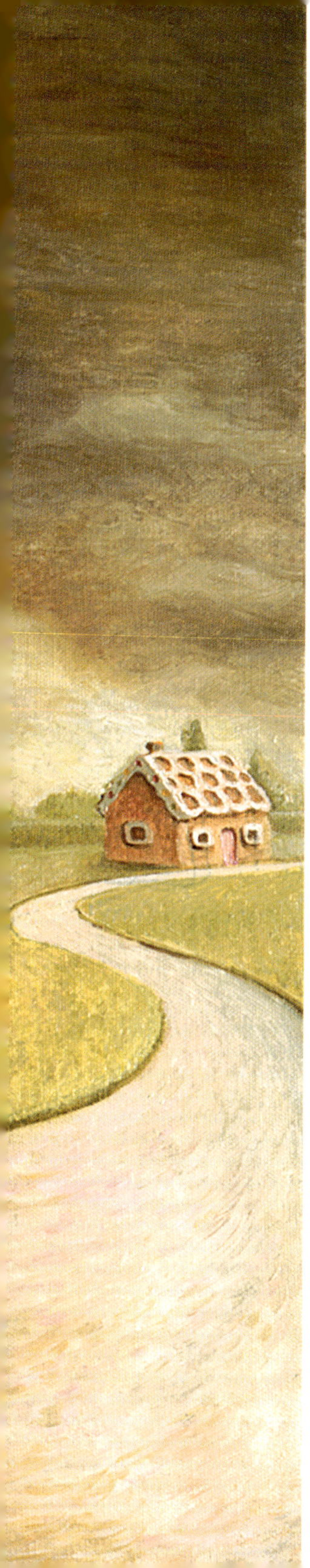

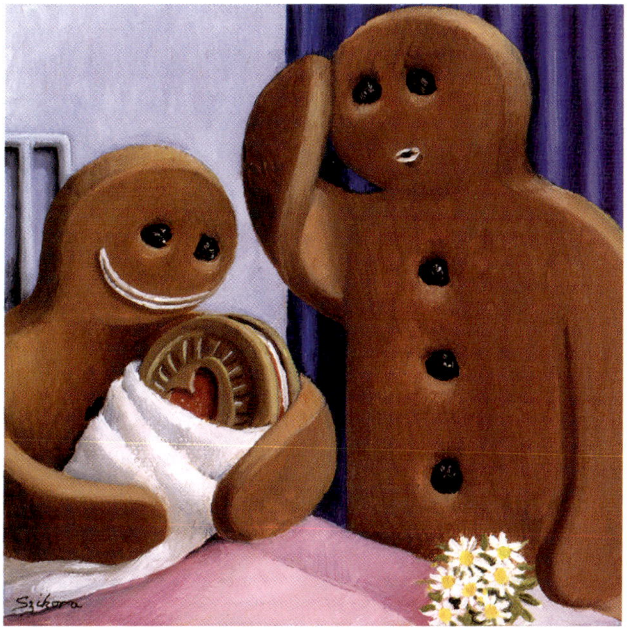

Of course, nowadays, many gingerbread families are more diverse. Every biscuit is at home in a multi-confectional society and lives peacefully alongside (sometimes even falling in love with) non-gingerbread.

Yums, Tums...

Gingerbread are usually vegetarian but they do like to have people for dinner on special occasions.

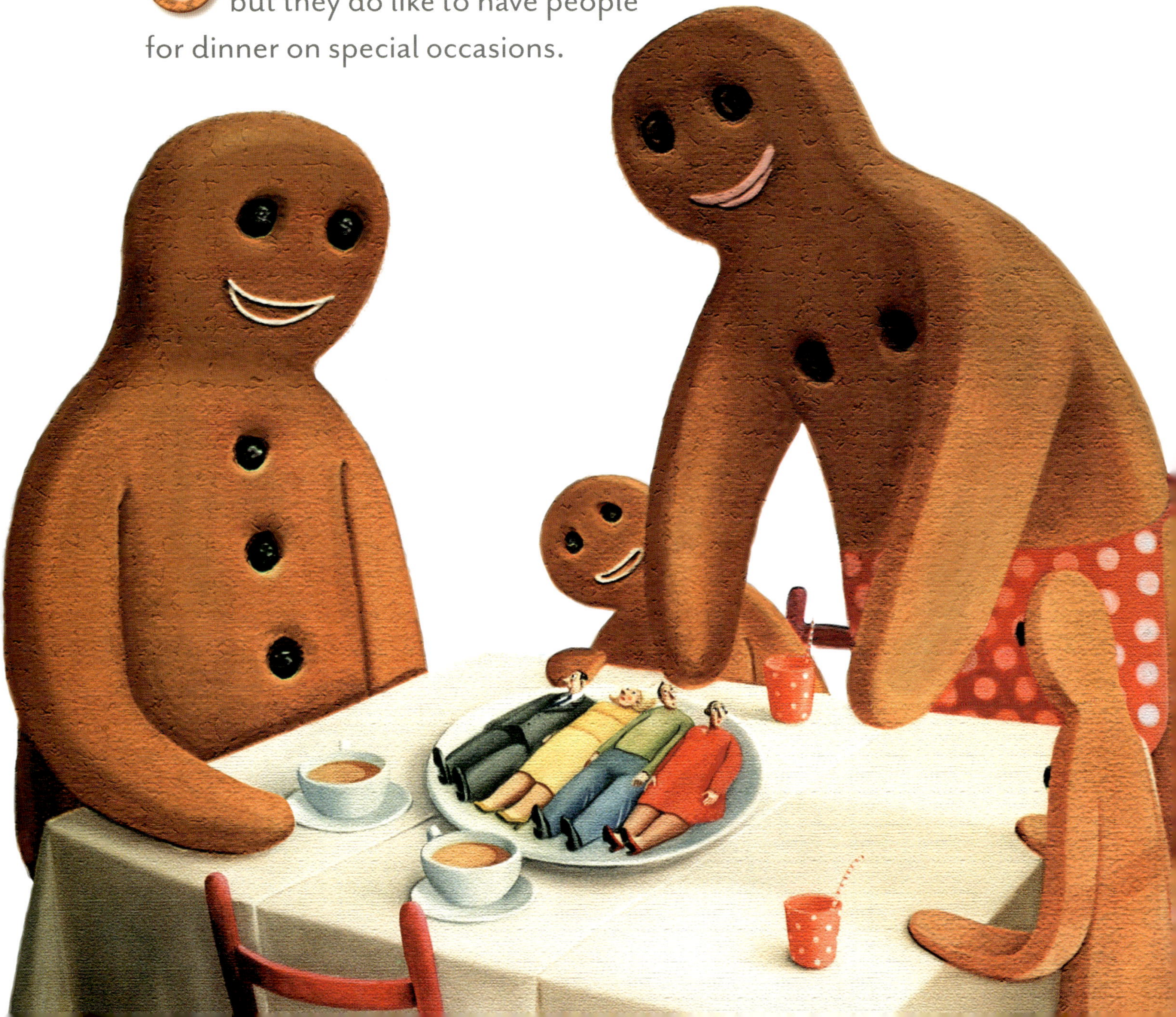

Sometimes things can go badly wrong and a rogue biscuit may get the urge to eat other biscuits.

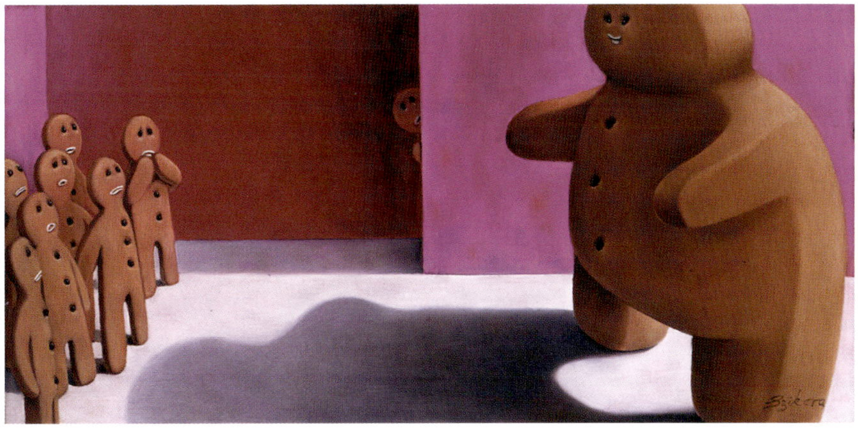

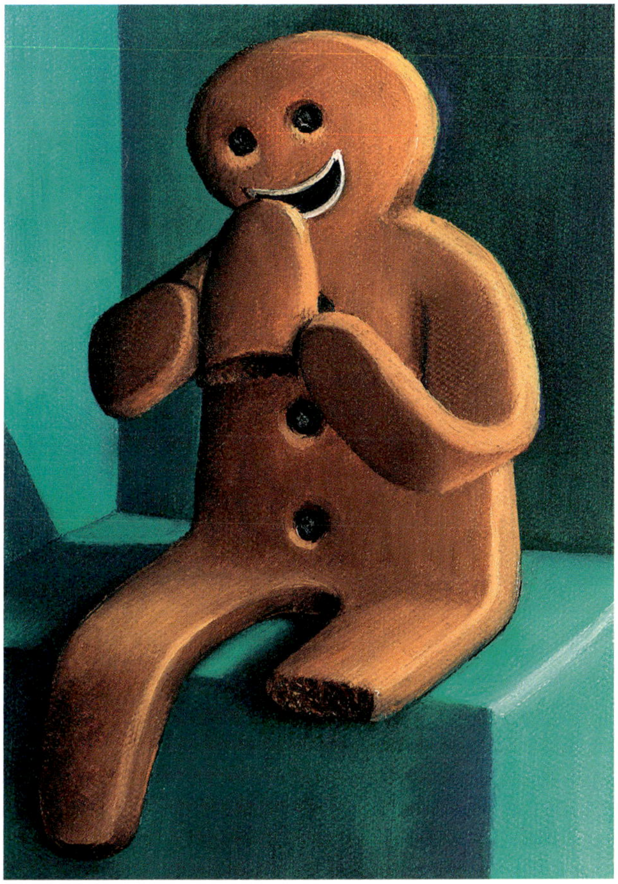

Even worse is a rare and tragic condition known as McVitivirus, which causes gingerbread to eat themselves. But there's no need for panic; they will harmlessly disappear into their own tummies.

...and Crumbs!

Health and safety hazards include the innocent looking cup of tea...

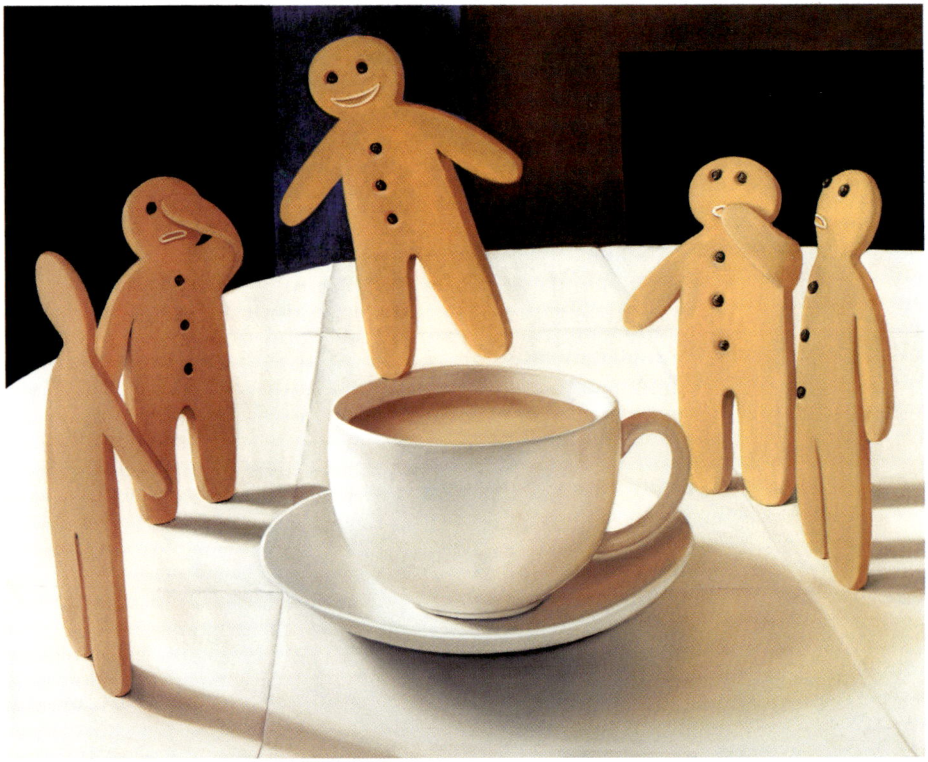

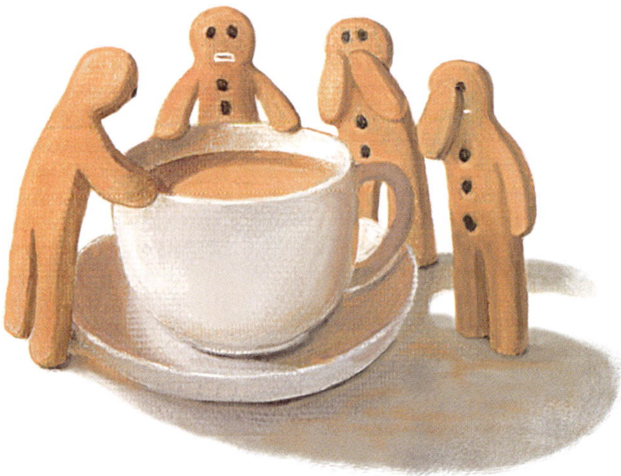

... although this is only a problem for foolish little biscuits.

Other hazards include damp conditions which can lead to acute limpness and the potential to catch a cold. Sneezing can prove disastrous for gingerbread.

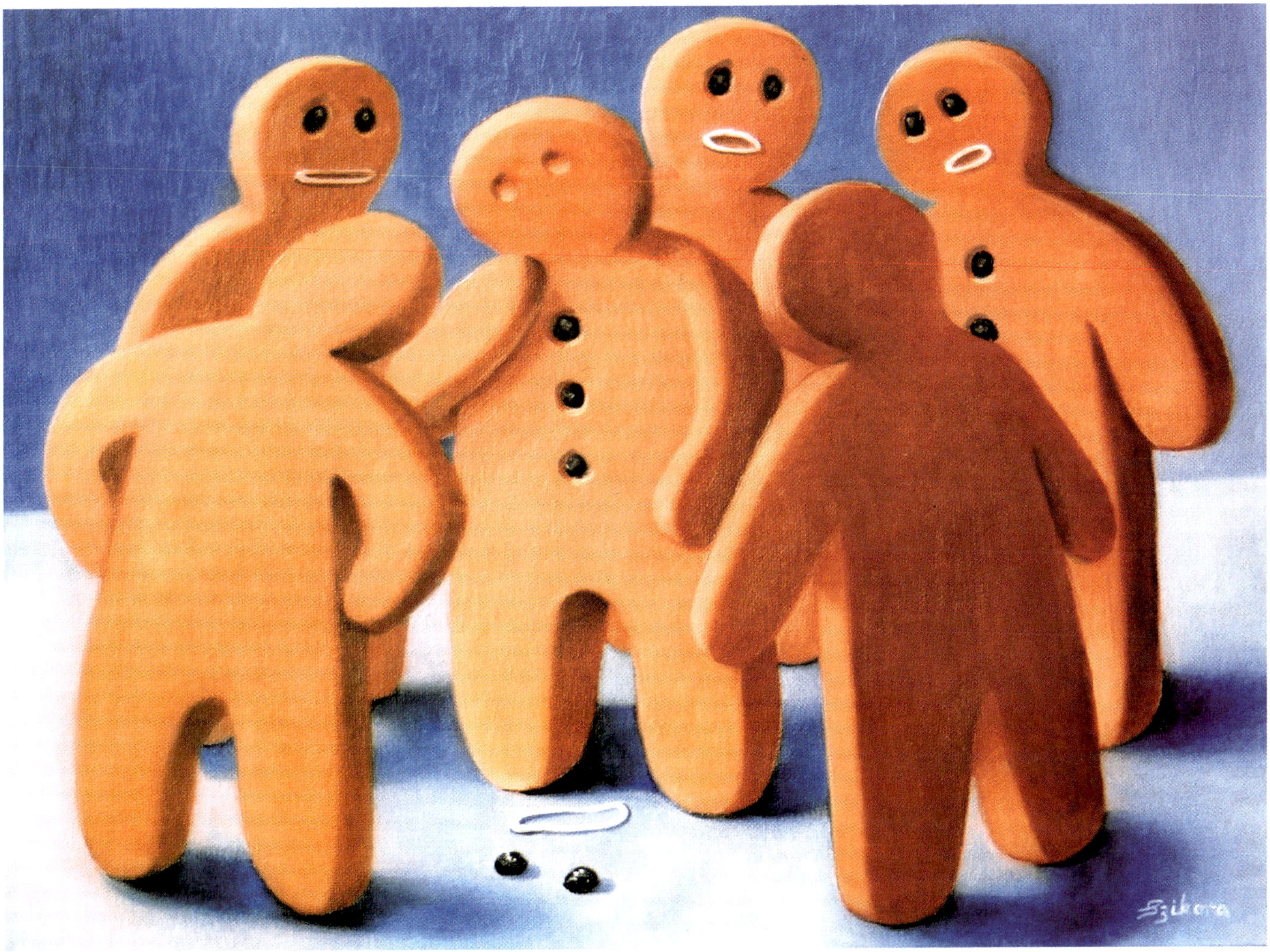

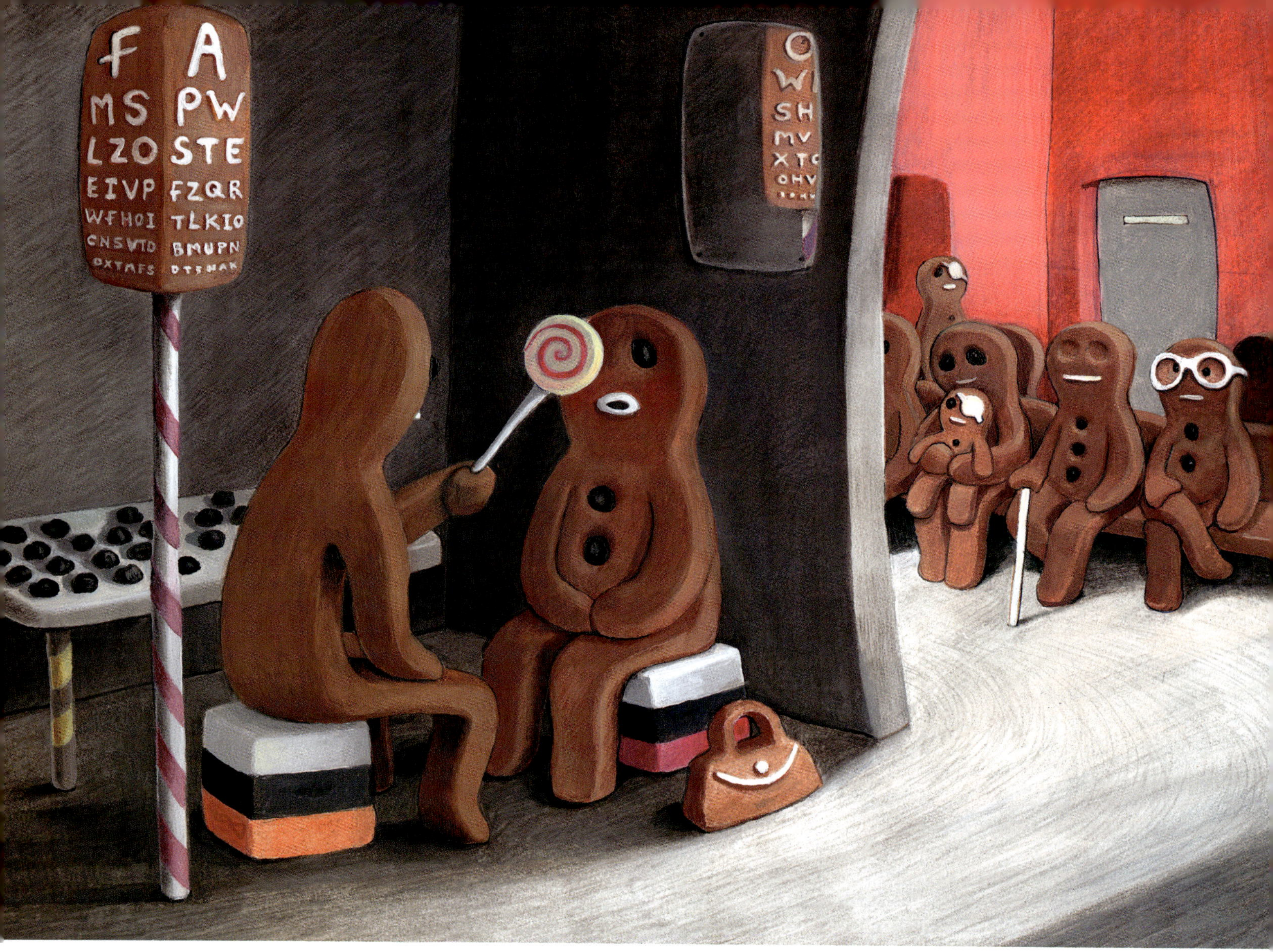

Brittle and accident prone, gingerbread sometimes need to visit specialist clinics for minor injuries and cosmetic treatments, such as raisin replacements.

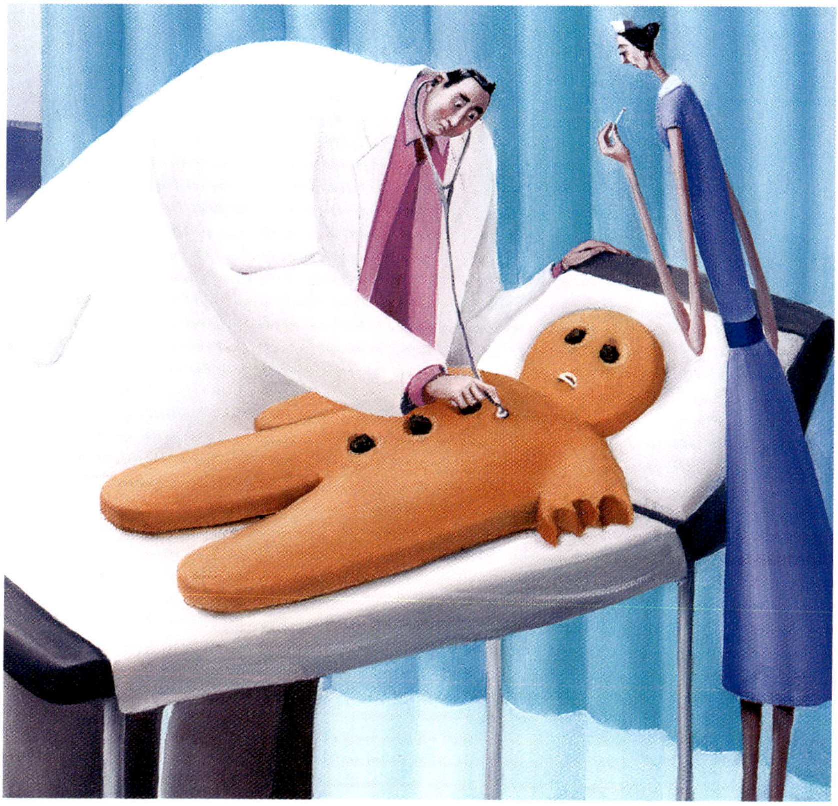

If medical attention becomes necessary, there are some kind and sympathetic human doctors.

For biscuits with more serious injuries, transplant surgery is available.

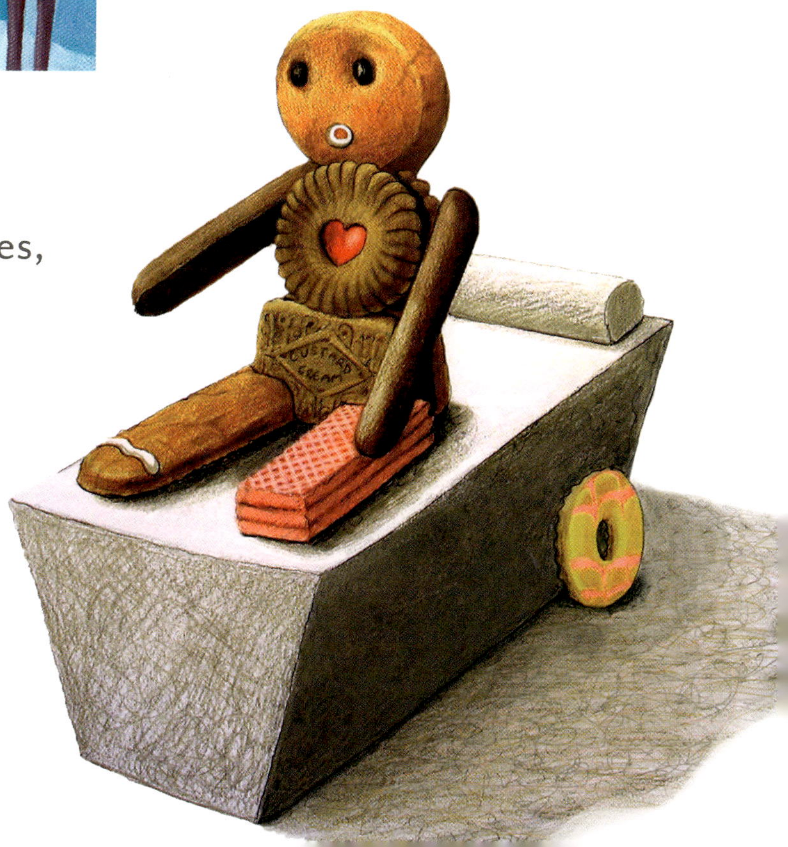

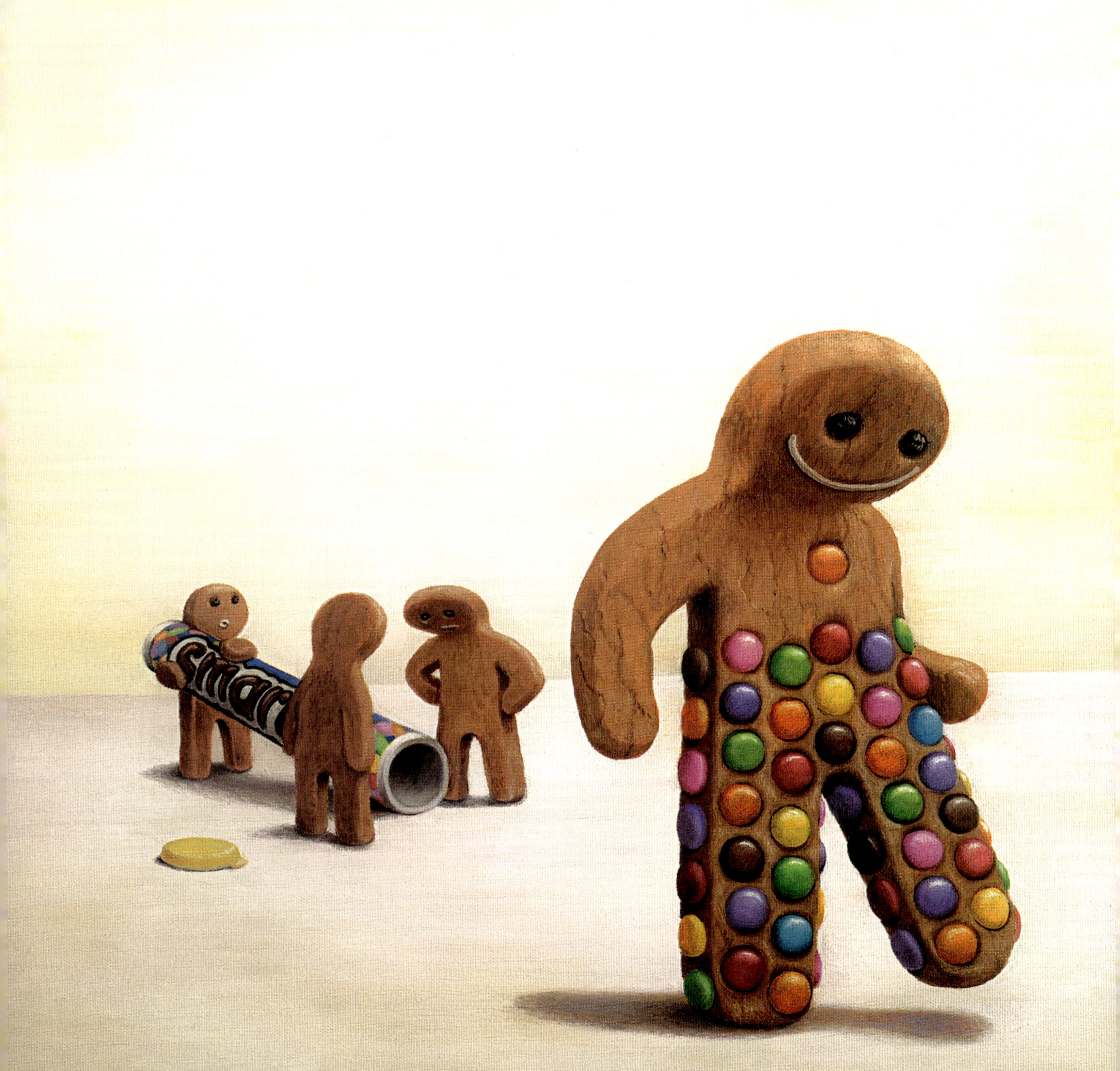
Smar

A Taste of the High Life

Fashion design is a booming industry. Currants and raisins are seen as too formal by younger gingerbread and creative new looks are regularly launched on the catwalk.

This on-trend biscuit isn't just cool but 'iced hot' in his chic smartypants.

When it comes to glamour, Hollywood in the 1930s takes the biscuit and two of its brightest stars were Ginger Snap and Bread Astaire.

They first met on the set of Busby Berkeley's *Teatime Assortment of 1929*, before going on to star in many films, including *I'll Eat My Hat!* and *Bourbon at the Sorbonne*.

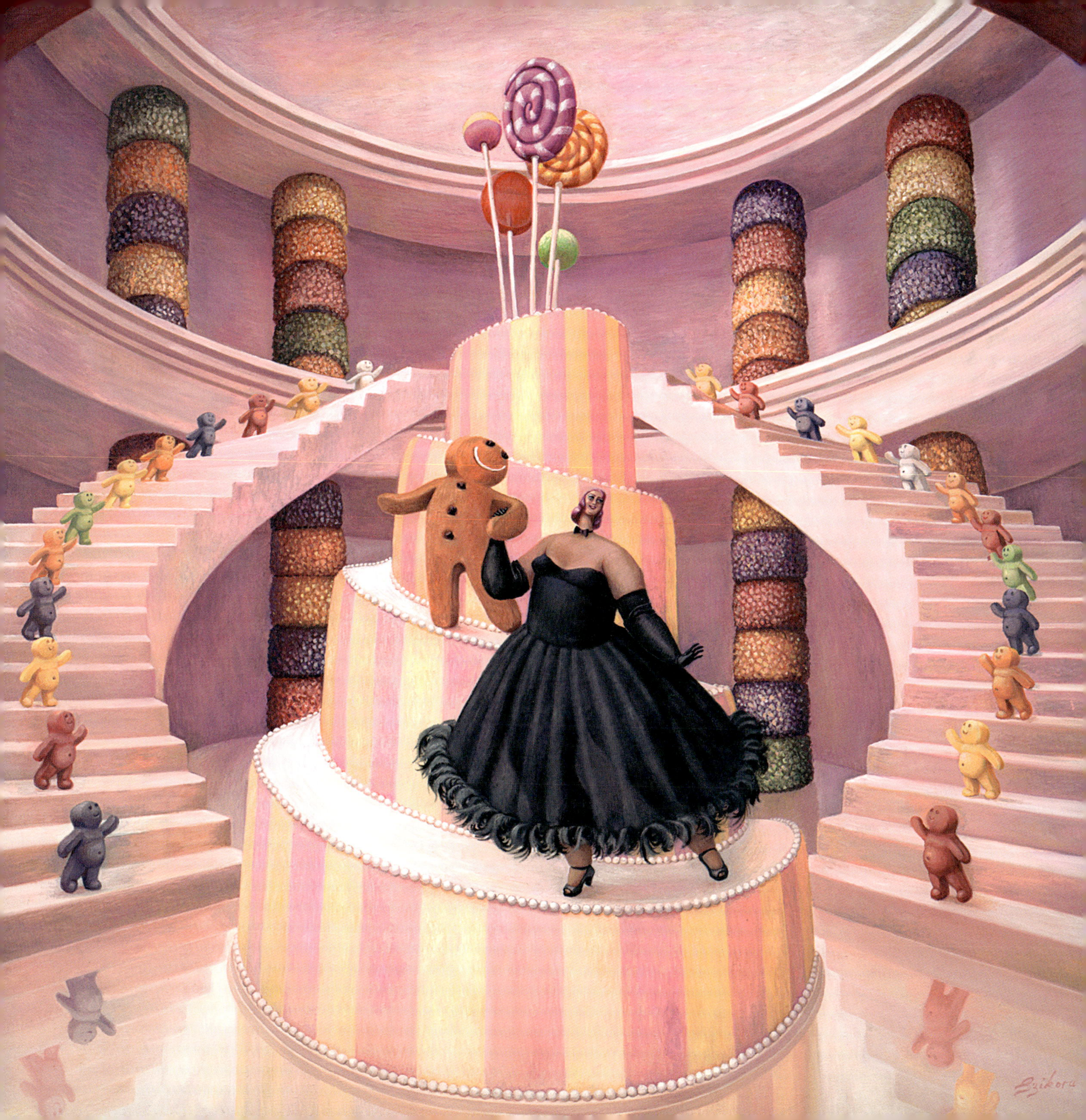

The collective noun for gingerbread is a 'gobble'.

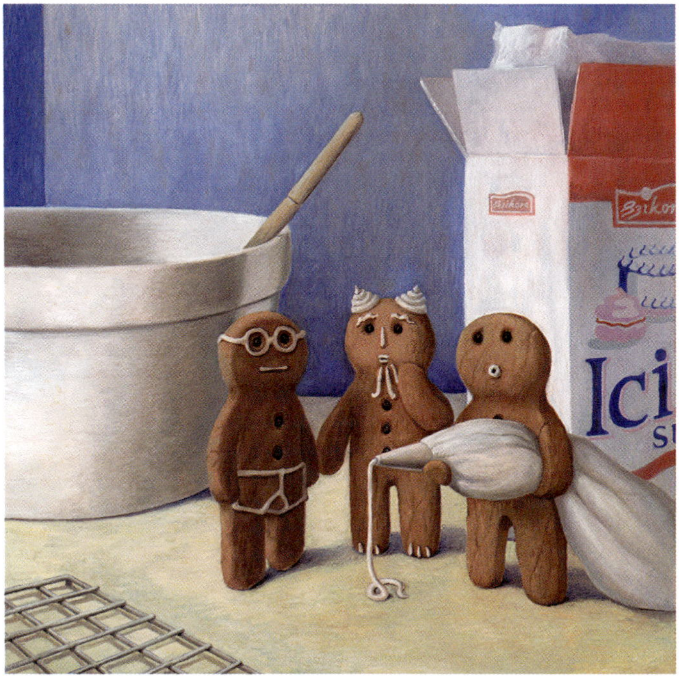

Naturally sociable, gingerbread love company but they can be very mischievous in gobbles. I found these three in my kitchen late one night. They were a bit hyperactive so I gently coaxed them into an old shoe box and they soon settled down.

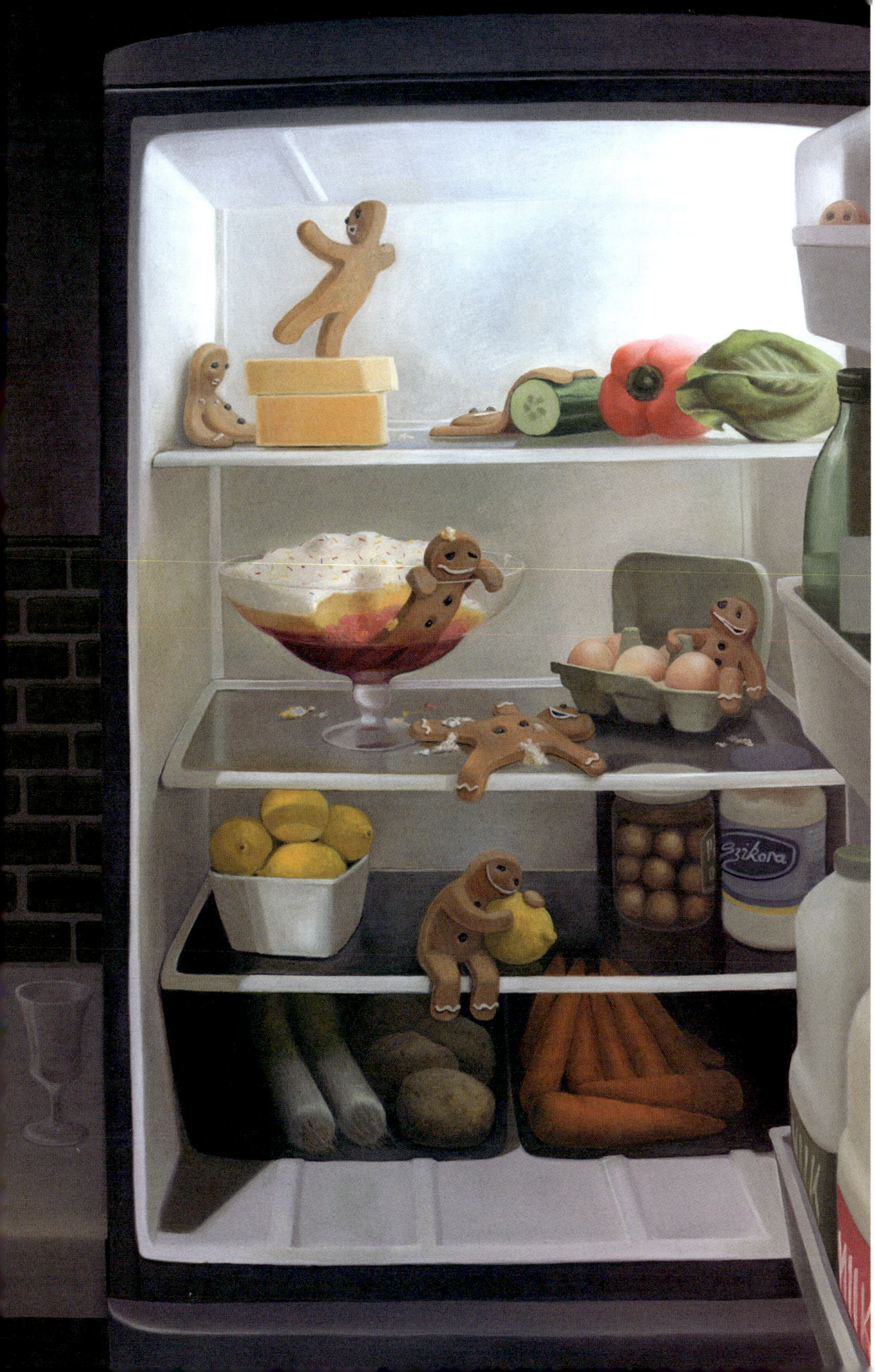

Gingerbread can fall
victim to worrying,
human vices.
An unattended
sherry trifle is just
asking for trouble.

Outrageous behaviour
should never be
encouraged. Drinks
and puddings should
be safely stored out of
harm's way.

If a gingerbread is caught being extra naughty he could get into deep trouble. I was the courtroom artist during the trial of a biscuit freedom fighter known as 'The Breakaway'. His crime was to help thousands of captive gingerbread escape from bakeries across London.

The Breakaway was found guilty and sentenced to three years behind bars.

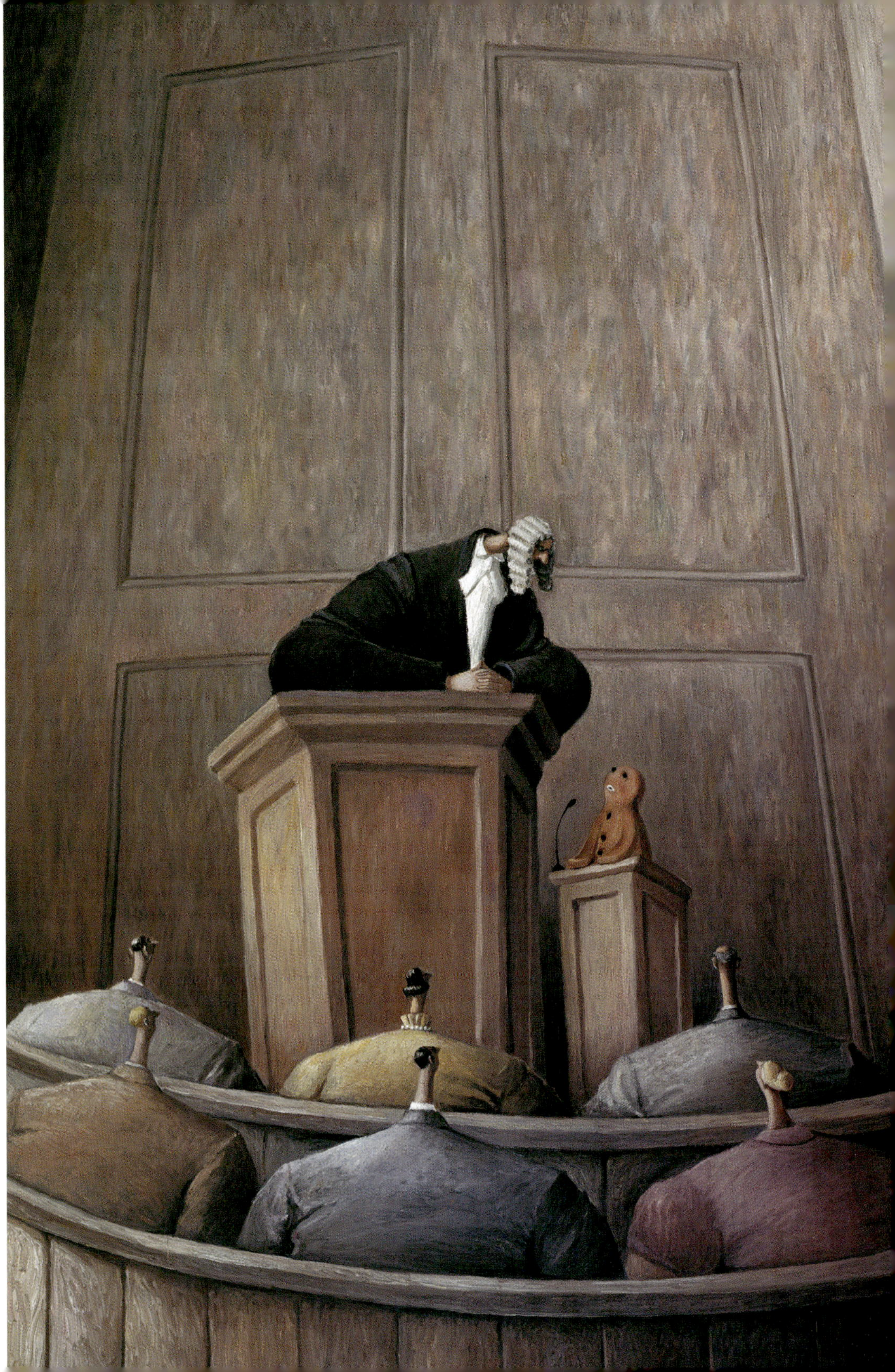

Sending gingerbread to prison is a harsh punishment indeed, mainly because they very rarely harm anyone and are always very, very sorry for their naughtiness.

It's a waste of time anyway as gingerbread are excellent escapologists. The Breakaway disappeared from his cell after only four hours and is still on the run.

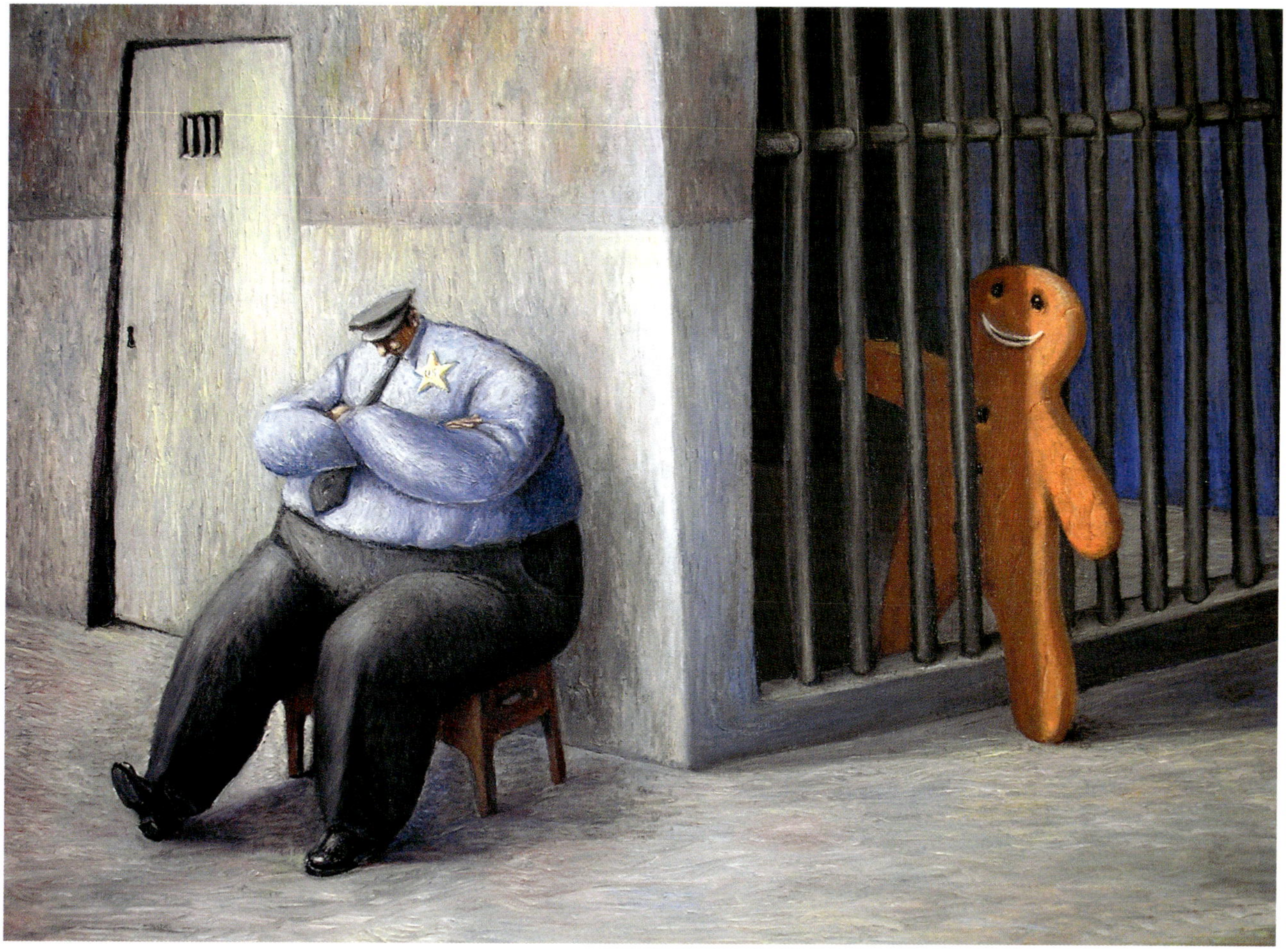

Gingerbread At Work...

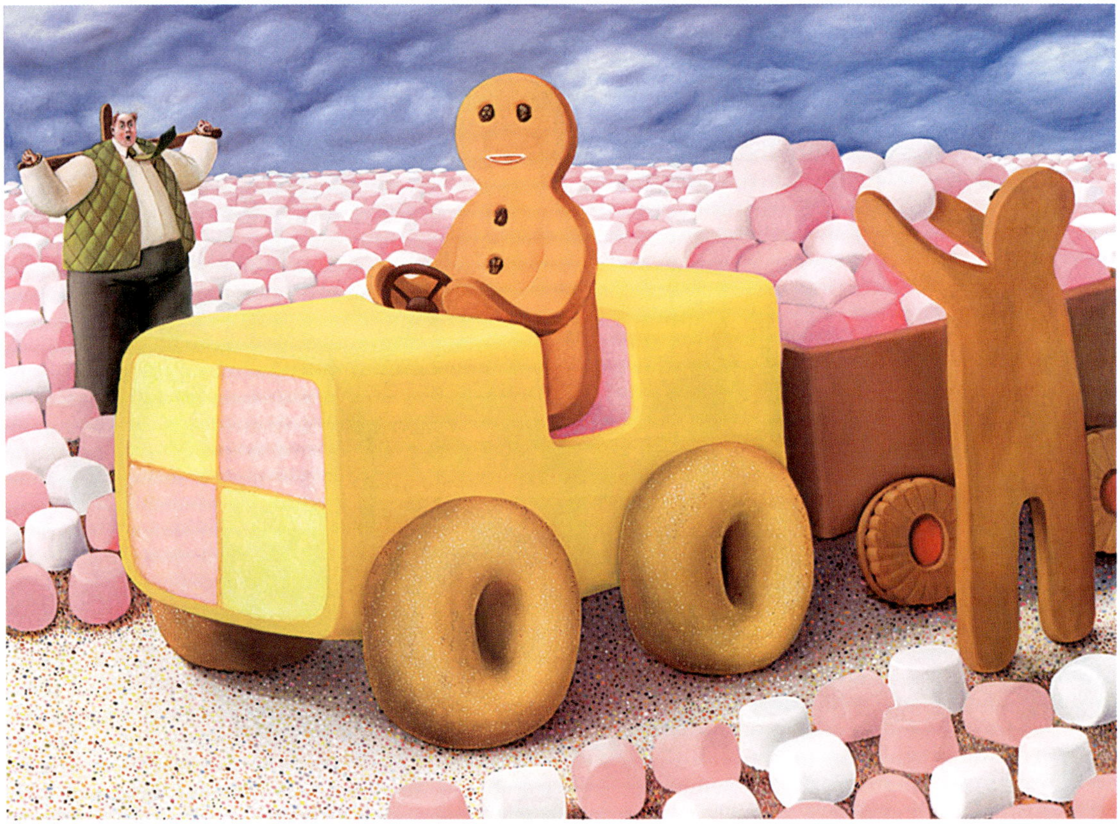

Gingerbread are known to be hard workers and this has led some humans to exploit them.

Greedy, landowning marshmallow farmers historically used biscuits as cheap labour until 1905, when a group known as the 'Bolshebiks' organised a revolution to overthrow them. Nowadays, gingerbread do all kinds of jobs.

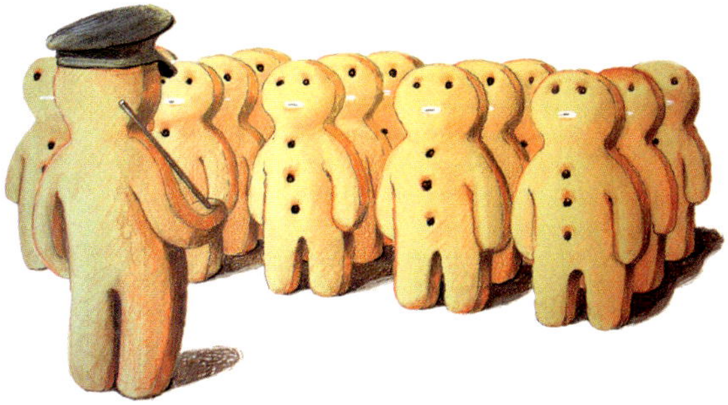

They have been known to join the military forces, though they are anti-war and not very effective in armed combat. Useless in fact.

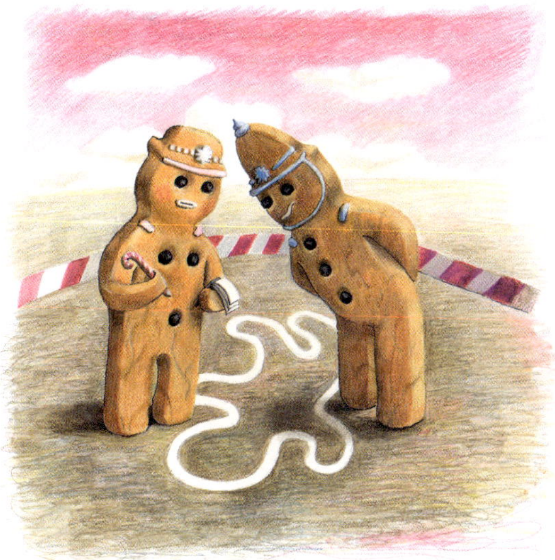

Gingerbread are much better at solving crime and Scotland Yard often ask ginger officers to help with difficult cases.

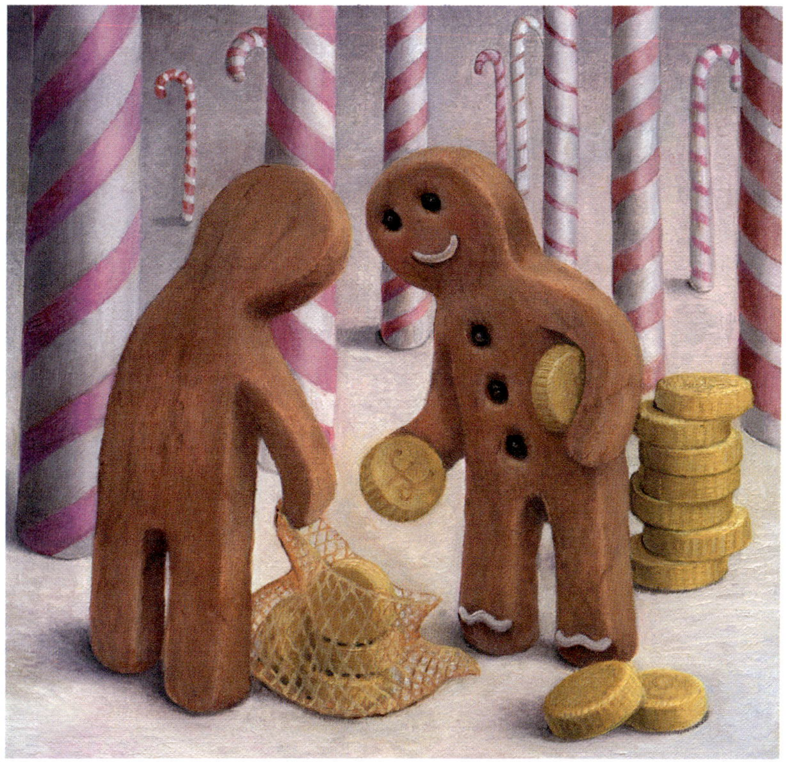

Banker biscuits, or 'breadheads', are responsible for minting the chocolate coins that you find in your Christmas stocking.

...and At Play

Gingerbread play hard too. Among the many activities they enjoy, musical pastimes are particularly popular. What humans don't realise about gingerbread is that their voices range from a deep velvety baritone to a tinkly soprano. However, they do struggle to play instruments on account of having no fingers.

A couple of years ago, I attended a performance of the opera *The Biscuit of Seville* by The London Choral Society. I couldn't believe my ears.

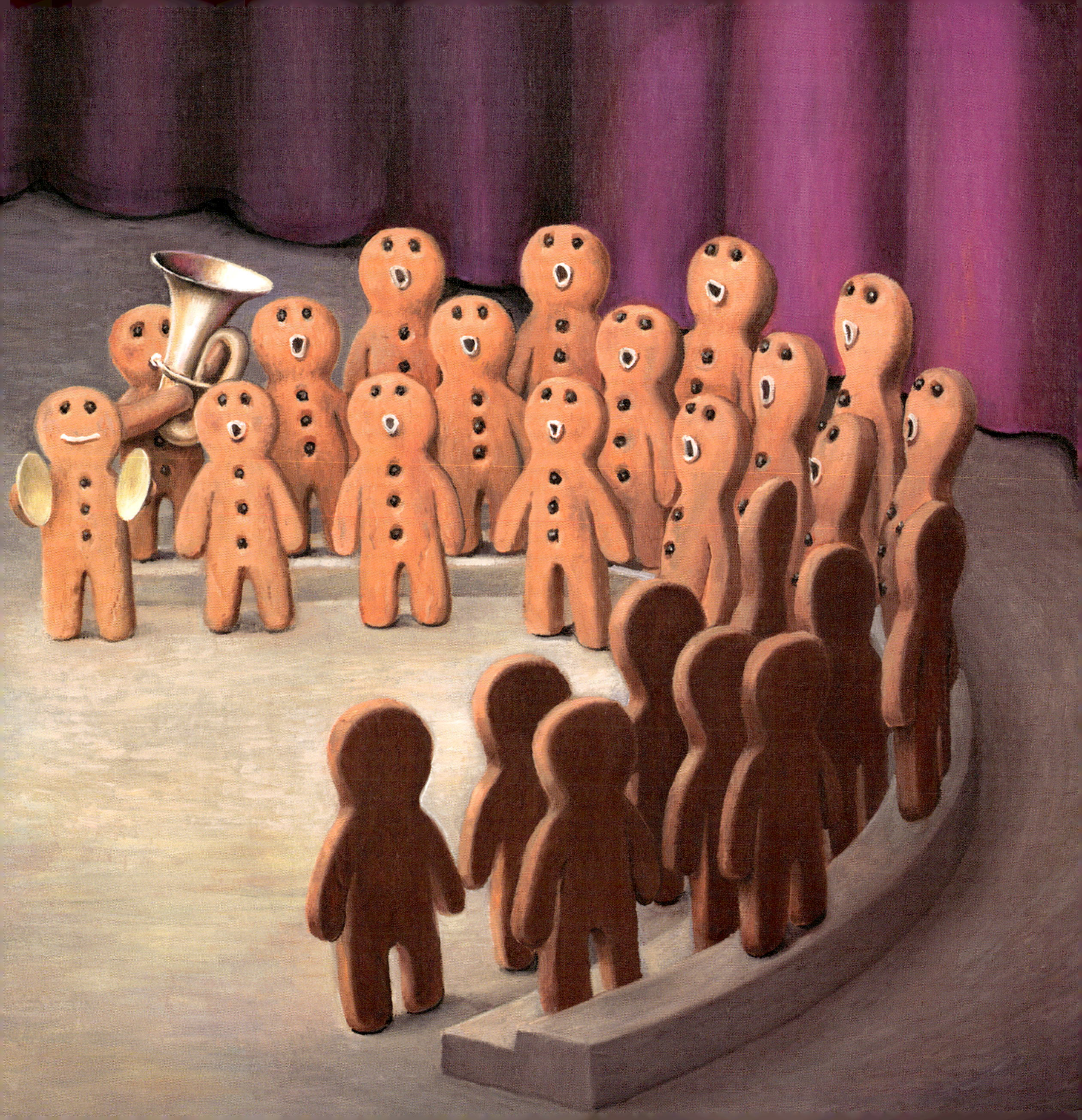

International Gingerbread

Budget airline *Gingerwings* has made it possible for biscuits to travel the world.

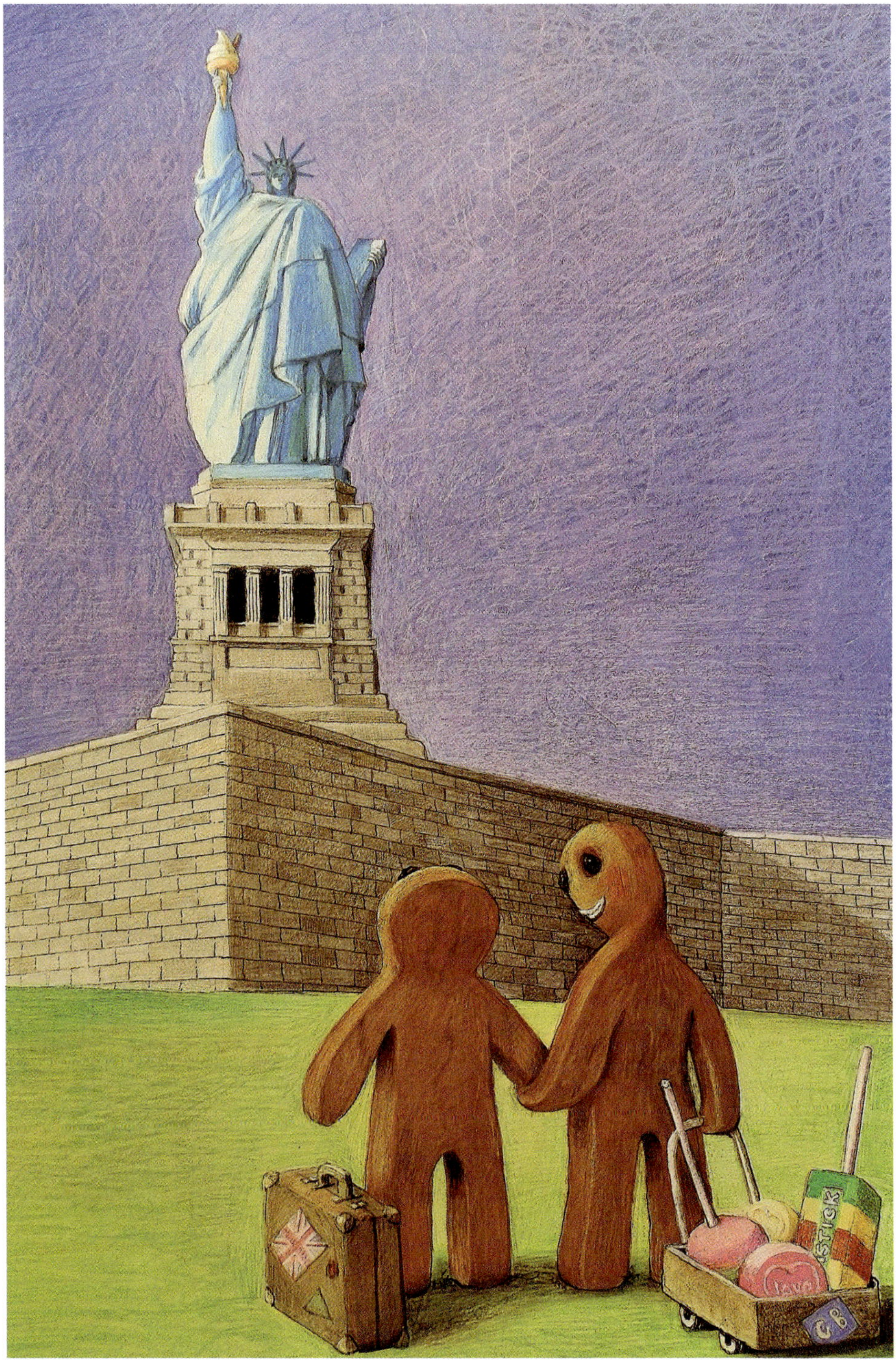

They love to take holiday snaps in
the most exotic and romantic places,
imagining themselves as a beautiful
Princess or an Emperor biscuit.

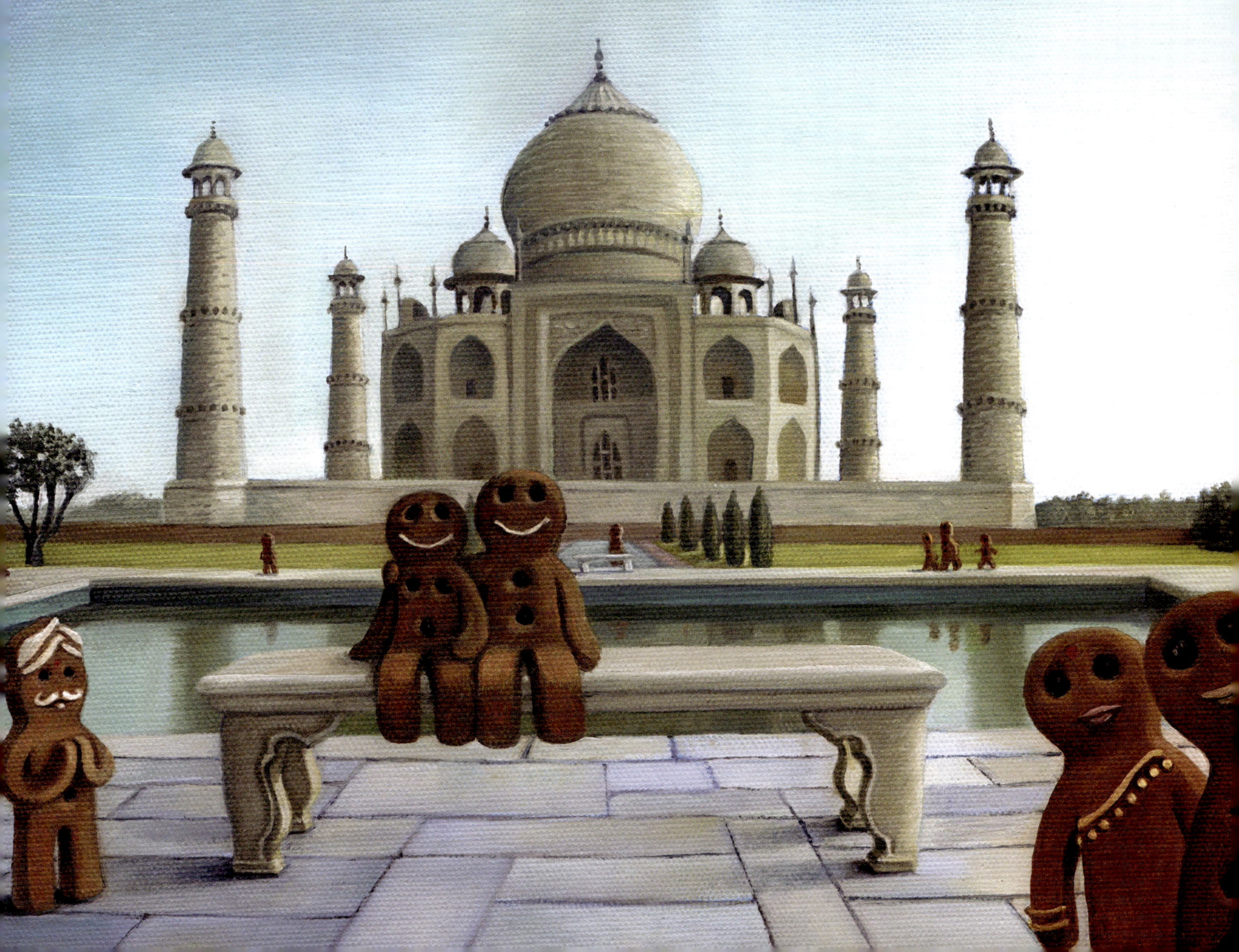

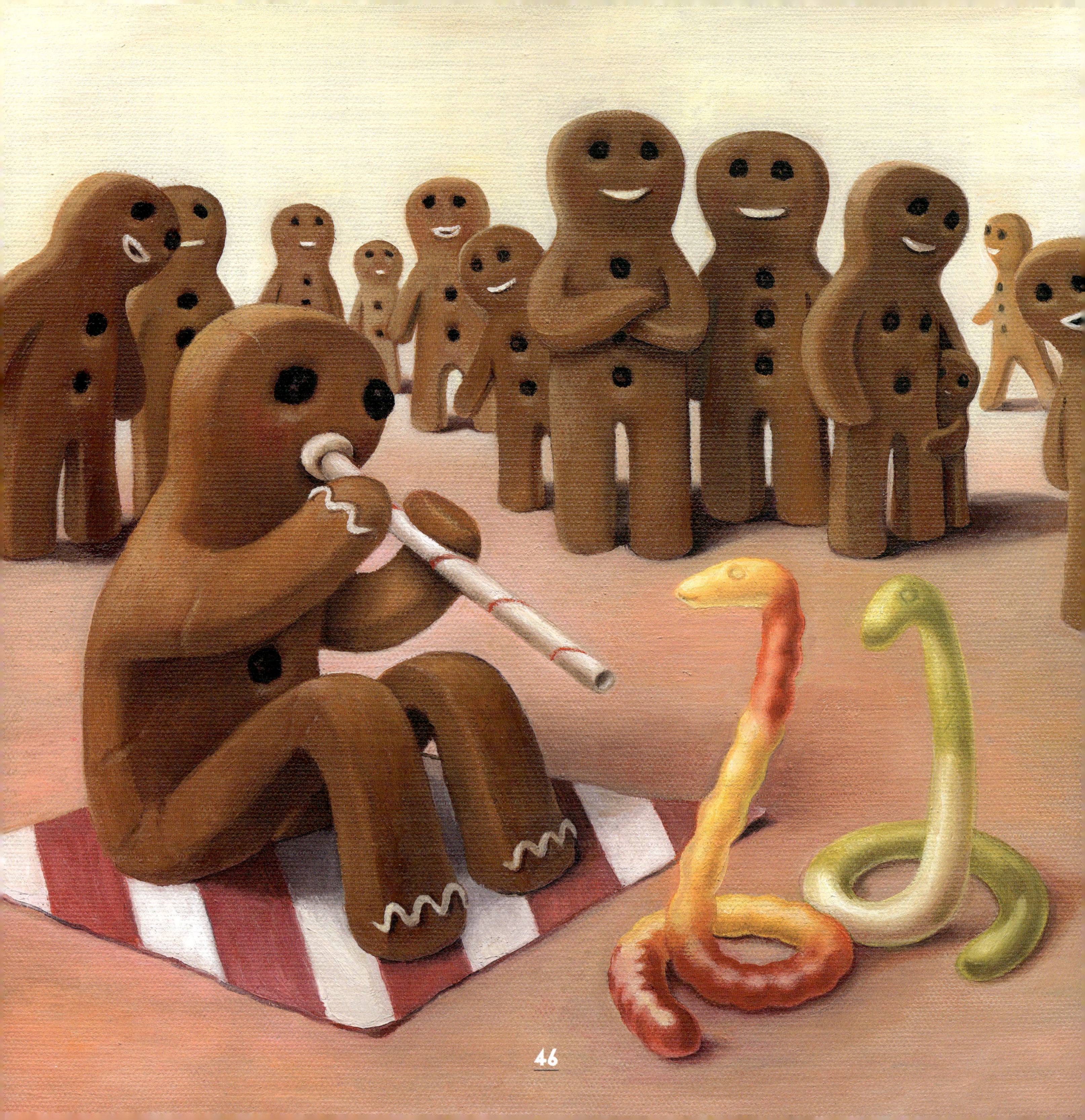

Some gingerbread who travel to exotic lands have discovered a talent for jelly snake charming. Fizzy snakes are known to be the most dangerous and are left alone.

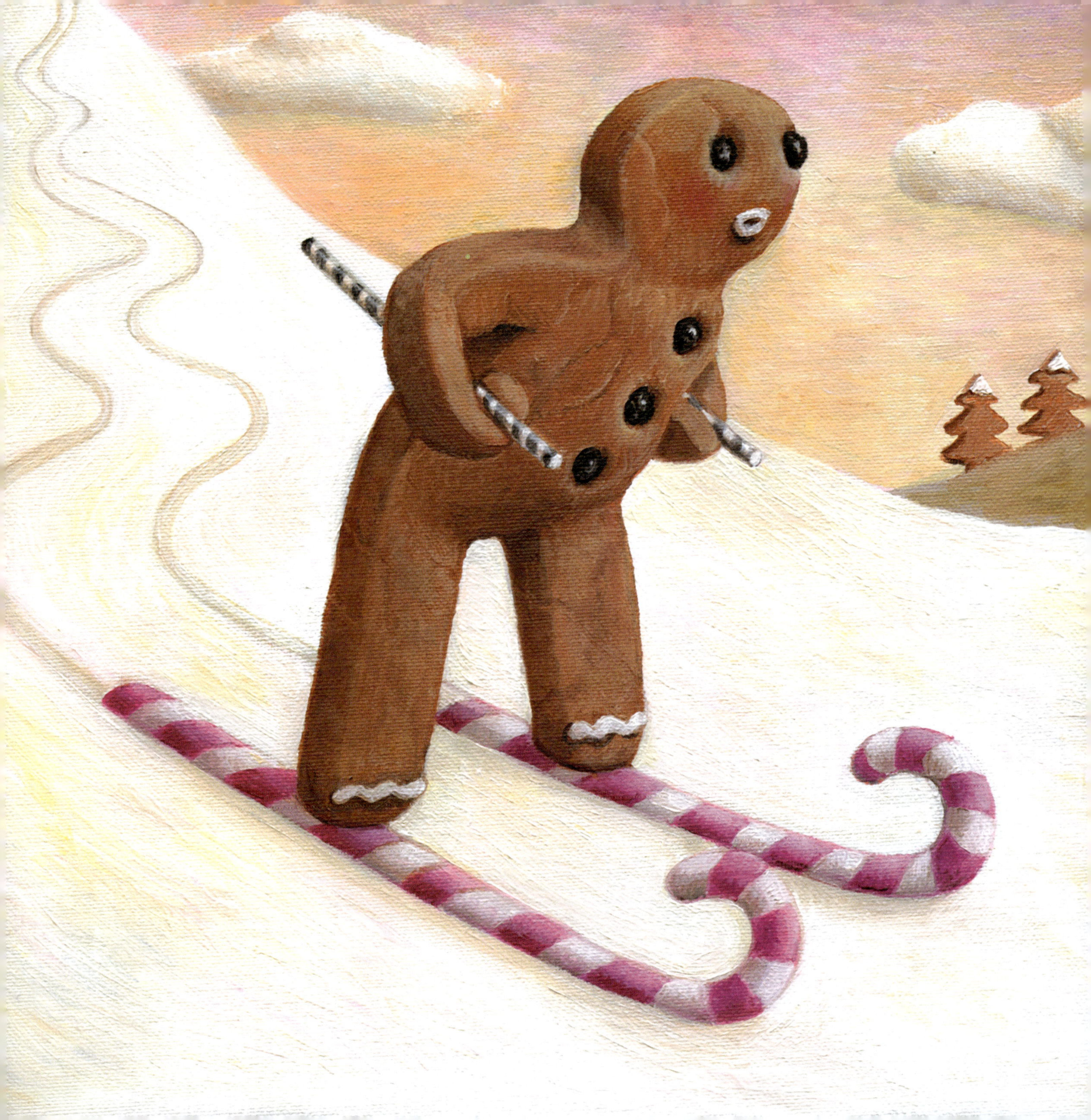

Skiing is NOT a sensible hobby due to the obvious risks, but there are a few thrill-seeking biscuits, commonly known as 'gingernuts'. These are not to be confused with the circular (and less nutty) biscuit of the same name.

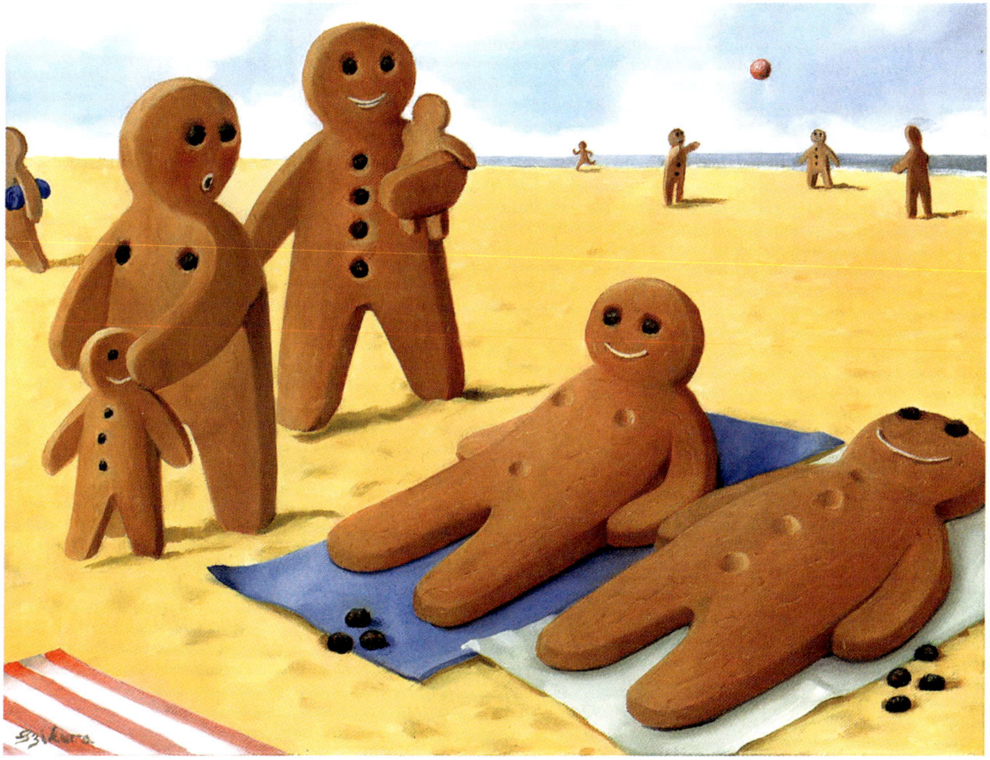

But of all gingerbread pastimes, resting and relaxing are the most popular. Naturist gingerbread are even more relaxed than others, willing to throw modesty to the wind and drop their currants.

Gingerbread Shelf Life

If a gingerbread has been lucky, he or she will survive natural breakage and escape the human jaws of death.

No longer young and moist, the older biscuit has acquired something important and valuable which he can share: wisdom. Young confectionery and baked goods alike are enthralled by an old biscuit's war stories and how he very nearly lost a leg in the Blitz because of sugar rationing.

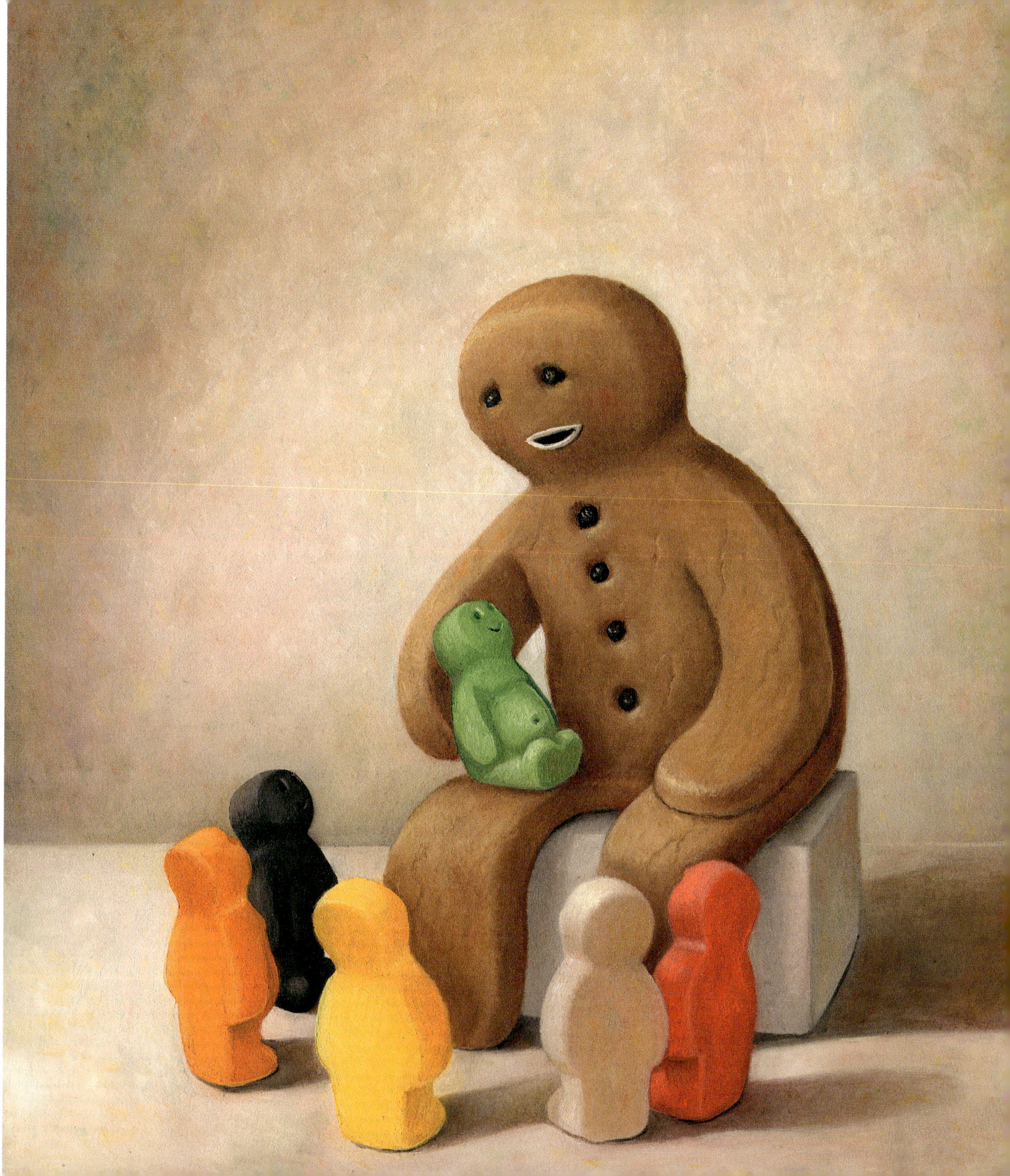

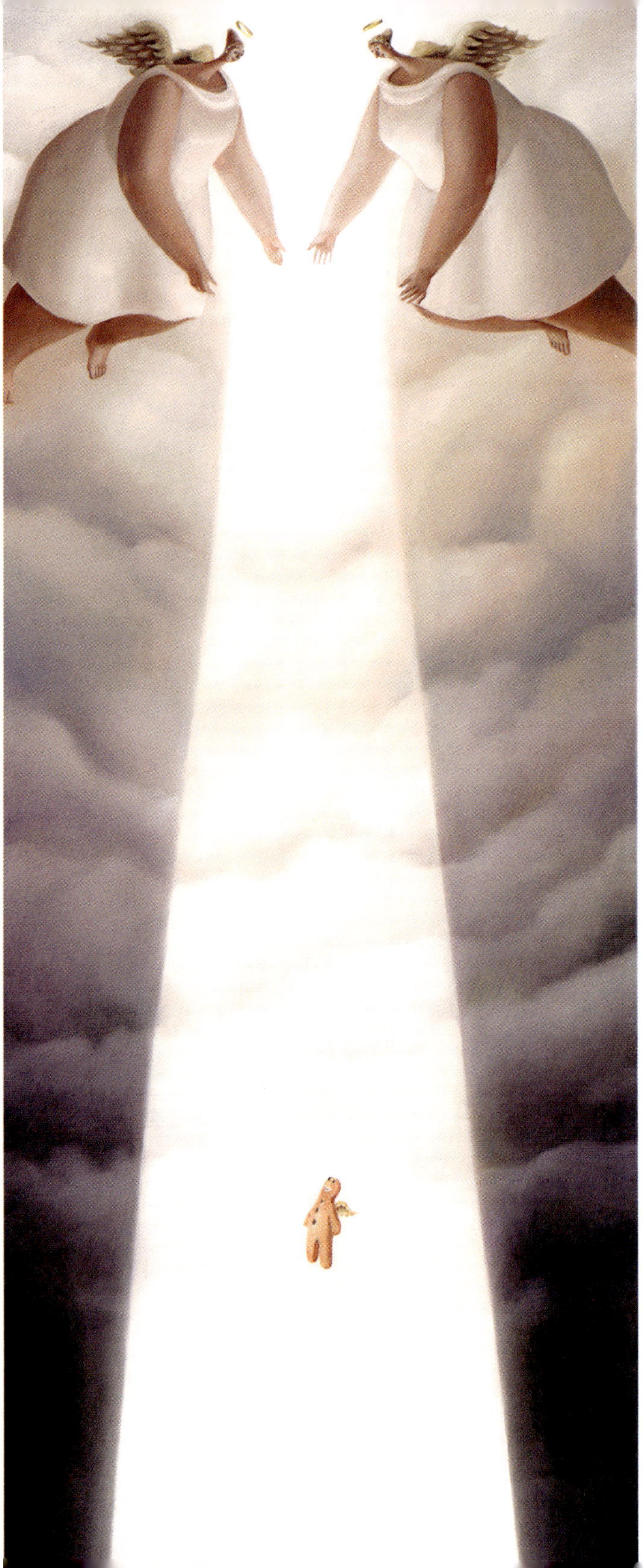

When a gingerbread biscuit is finally ready to die, he will drift away peacefully.

Sometimes gingerbread donate their raisins to medical science and leave their bodies for use in the base of cheesecake.

GINGERBREAD FUTURE

On a recent trip to Japan, I was very excited to visit a secret laboratory where the highly advanced digital Robo-Biscuit 3000 is being developed. Everyone is sure to want one of these clever and useful biscuit machines – they can withstand hot tea and do the vacuuming!

It used to worry me that the human desire to eat lovely biscuits might send gingerbread to extinction, but they have always found a way to survive. Something tells me that this ancient, resilient little species is here to stay and will continue to move with the times.

Gingerbread might even take over the world one day. What a thought!

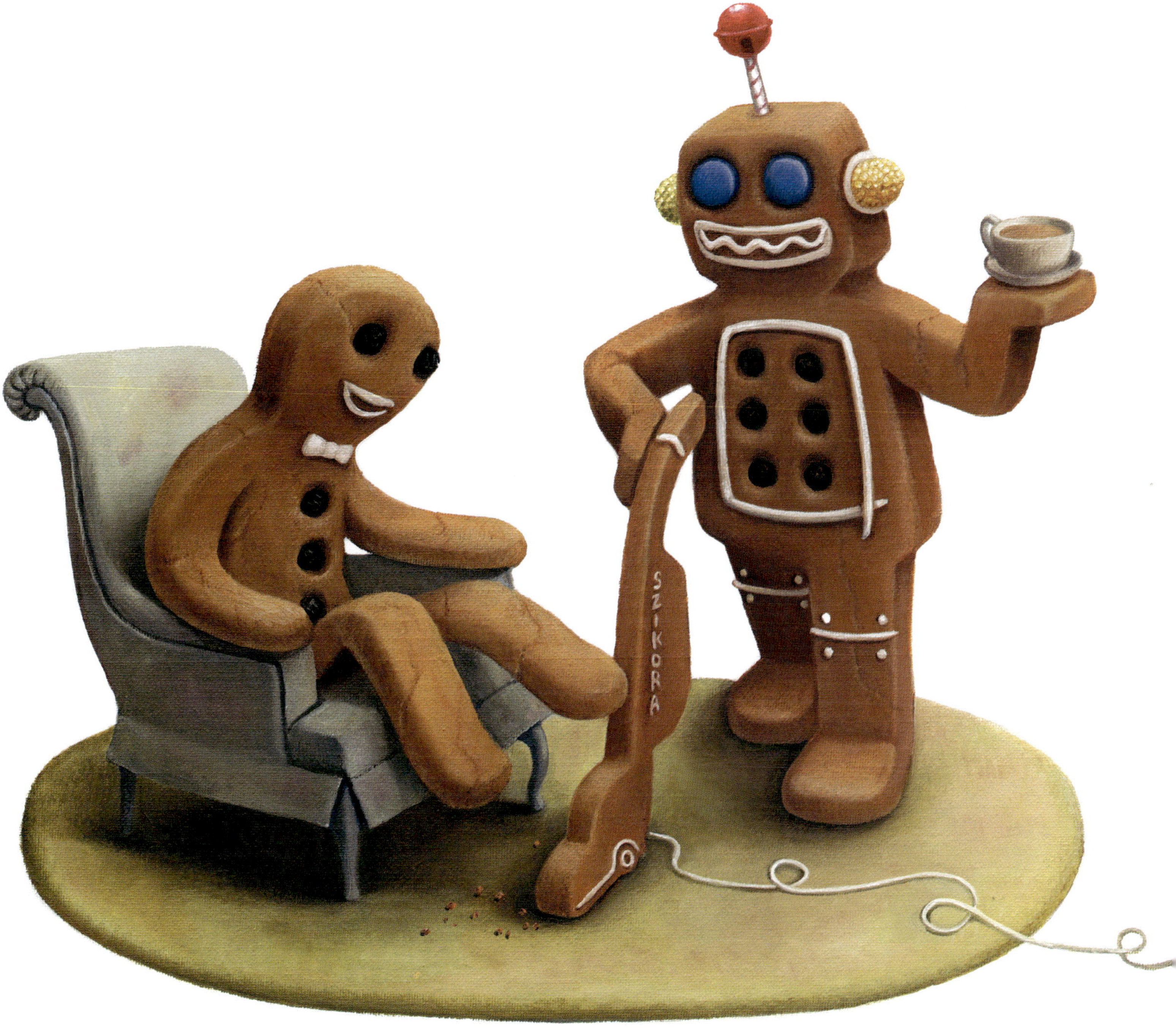
SZIKORA

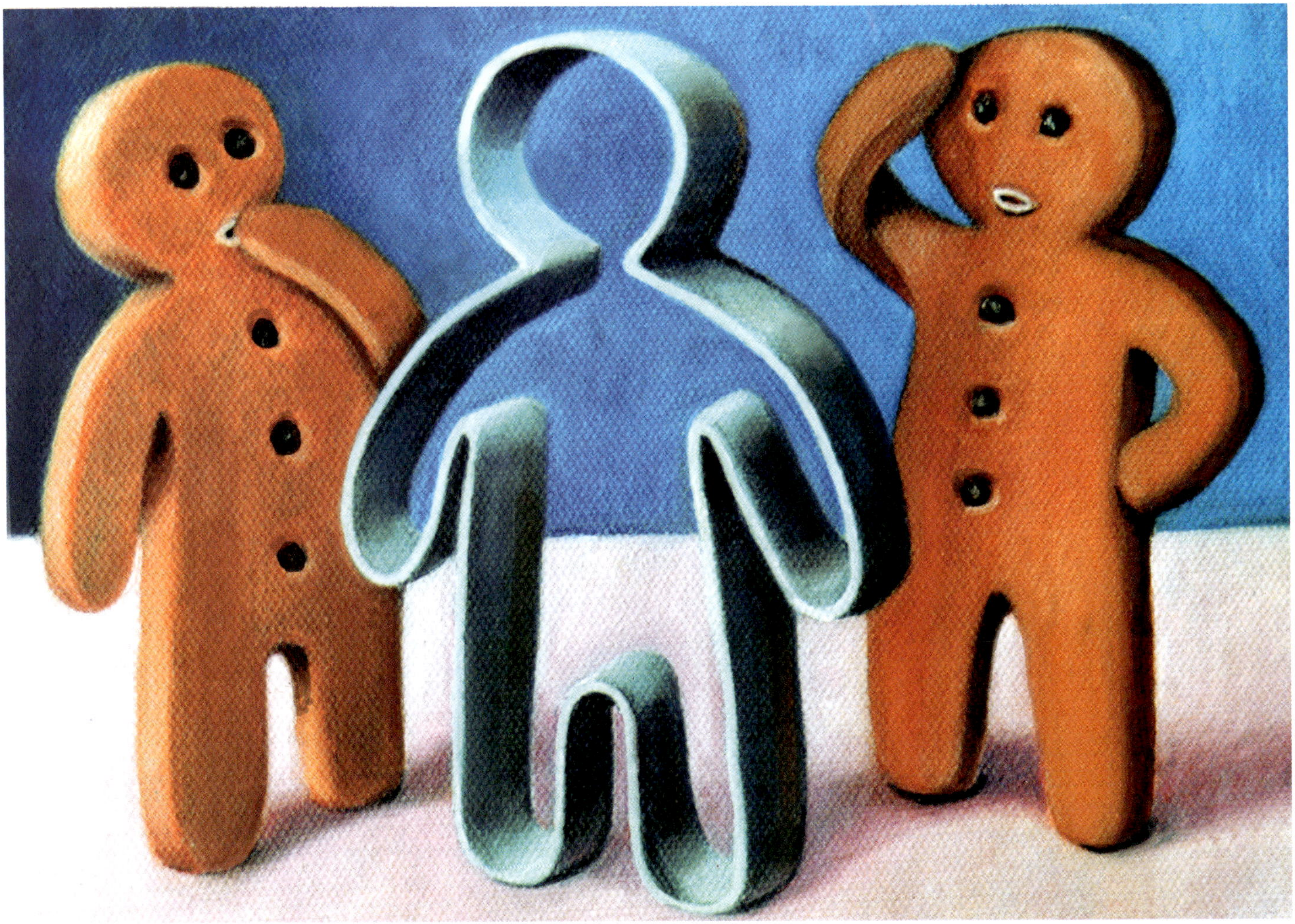

A new and controversial development in the world of gingerbread is cloning. Once the entire gingerbread genome has been mapped, scientists say it will be possible to create trays of identical gingerbread in the laboratory.
It may sound like science fiction, but 'designer gingerbread' is set to be the hot topic of the twenty-first century.

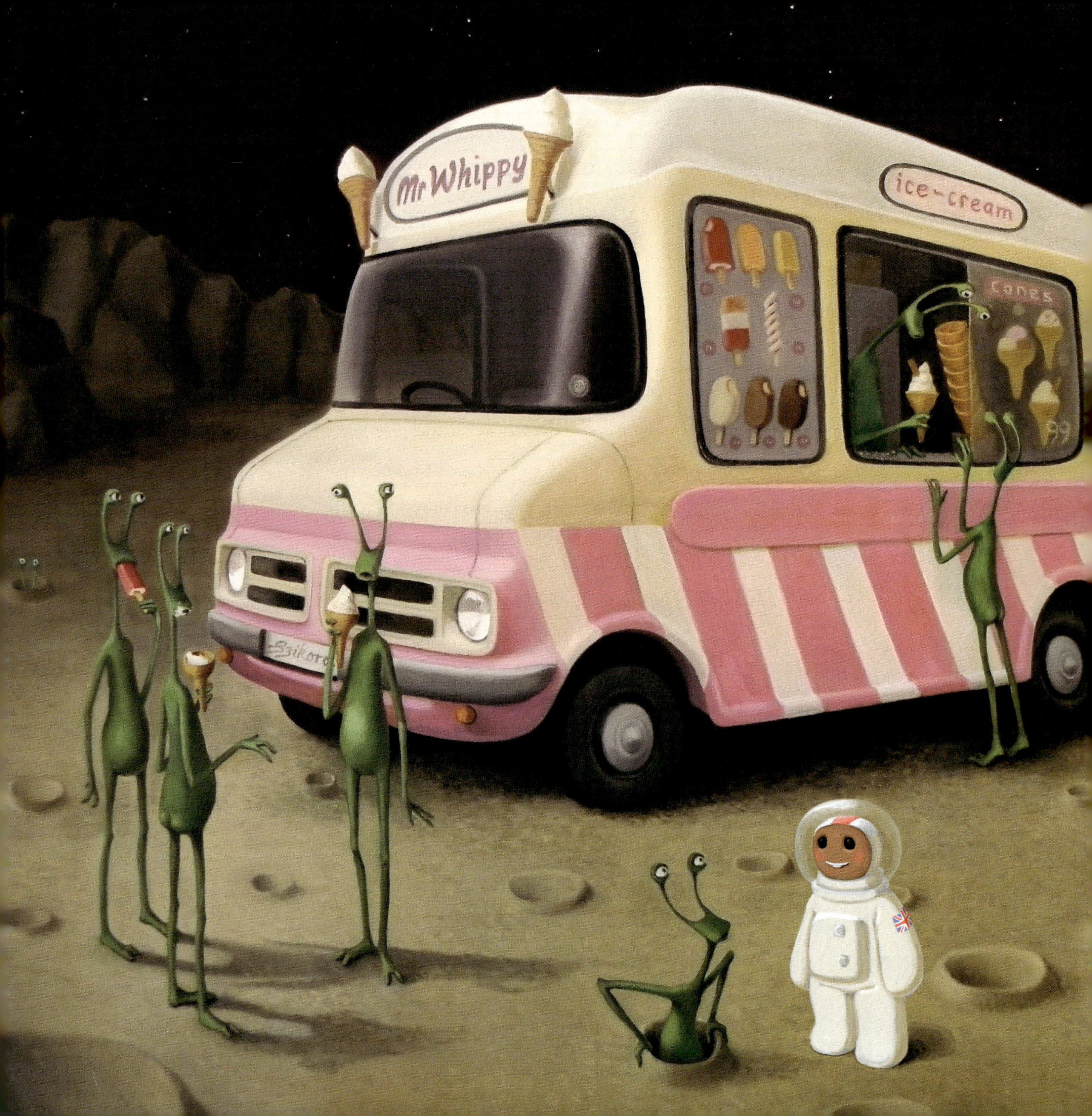
Mr Whippy
ice-cream
cones
99

Experiments aboard the Gingernational Space Station have proved that gingerbread can live happily in zero gravity. Any sponginess is easily remedied by a daily routine of 20 minutes on the treadmill followed by 10 minutes in the oven.

One day, gingerbread may take one small step to colonise the Moon or Mars, or even travel beyond our solar system in a giant leap for biscuitkind.

So dear reader,

There we have it. I do hope you've enjoyed my book and the next time you settle down for a nice cup of tea I wonder what biscuit you will choose to go with it - a Custard cream pershaps?

If you still want to eat gingerbread (and who could blame you), then at least remember to bite off his head first so that he doesn't have to watch as you eat his arms and legs.

Lots of love
Sarah-Jane Szikora
Biscuit explorer

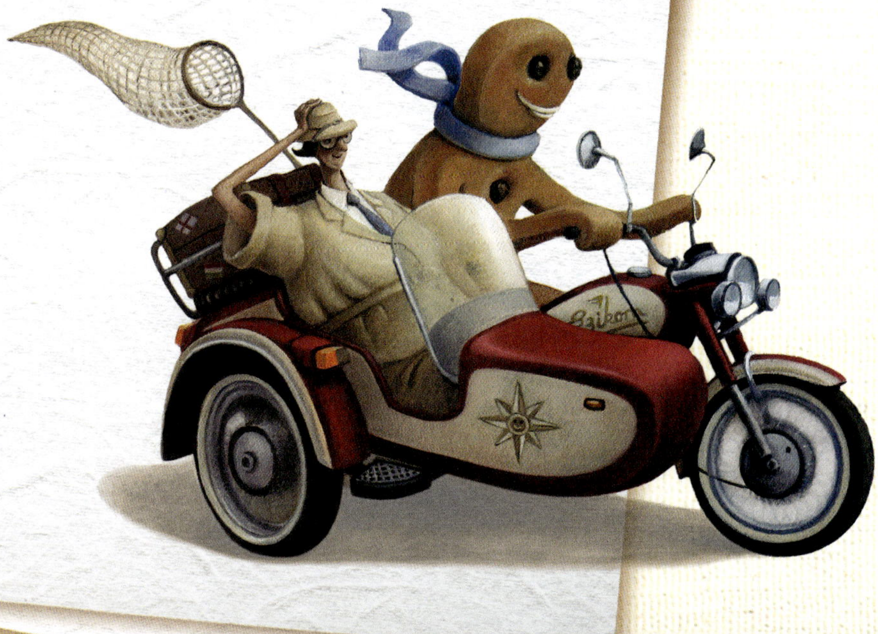

P.S. For my next adventure, I am heading off to the Amazon rainforest in search of an ancient and mysterious tribe of pygmy biscuits.
I'll send a postcard!